HIGHER CIVIL SERVANTS IN AMERICAN SOCIETY

A Study of the Social Origins, the Careers,
and the Power-Position of Higher Federal
Administrators

BY

REINHARD BENDIX

UNIVERSITY OF COLORADO STUDIES
Series in Sociology
No. I

GREENWOOD PRESS, PUBLISHERS
WESTPORT, CONNECTICUT

Library of Congress Cataloging in Publication Data

Bendix, Reinhard.
   Higher civil servants in American society.

   Reprint of the 1949 ed., published by the University
of Colorado Press, Boulder, in series: University of
Colorado studies; series in sociology, no. 1.
   Includes bibliographical references.
   1. United States--Officials and employees. 2. Civil
service--United States. 3. Government executives--
United States. I. Title. II. Series: Colorado.
University. University of Colorado studies. Series in
sociology, no. 1.
JK691.B513 1974   301.44'92   73-17856
ISBN 0-8371-7265-9

Originally published in 1949 by University of Colorado
Press, Boulder

Reprinted with the permission of Colorado Associated
University Press

Reprinted in 1974 by Greenwood Press,
a division of Williamhouse-Regency Inc.

Library of Congress Catalogue Card Number 73-17856

ISBN 0-8371-7265-9

Printed in the United States of America

CONTENTS

PREFACE

This study is a revision of my doctoral dissertation, which was submitted to and accepted by the Department of Sociology, The University of Chicago, in partial fulfilment of the requirements for the degree, Doctor of Philosophy. I wish here to express my appreciation of the financial assistance received from the Social Science Research Committee at The University of Chicago for the purpose of making this study and to acknowledge my indebtedness to Professors Louis Wirth and Leonard D. White, both of The University of Chicago.

REINHARD BENDIX[*]

[*] Assistant Professor of Sociology, University of Colorado, 1946–1947; now Assistant Professor of Sociology and Social Institutions, University of California, Berkeley, California.

HIGHER CIVIL SERVANTS IN AMERICAN SOCIETY

CHAPTER I

BUREAUCRACY AND THE PROBLEM OF POWER*

The development of bureaucracy is popularly identified with the diminution of individual freedom. This identification has given rise to a series of denunciations of bureaucracy, ranging from the fear of an undue usurpation of power and of vested interest of officials to complaints about the waste of public funds, unnecessary red tape, and the lack of practical judgment on the part of government officials.[1]

Experts in the field of public administration have frequently selected their topics in response to such sentiments. They have focused their attention on such problems as those of judicial review, administrative discretion, the separation of powers, quasi-judicial procedures, and administrative efficiency. In effect, these studies have met specific allegations against an administration (and against any administration) with specific disclaimers or suggestions for improvement. Yet these disclaimers and suggestions have, in a sense, avoided the real issues underlying the compaints. Experts have attempted to formulate quasi-judicial procedures for administrative agencies, although the clamoring for judicial review by the critics of these agencies was prompted by a desire to curb their powers, not to improve their procedures.

This criticism does not deny the value of such studies in public administration, but calls attention to certain neglected problems in this field. Clearly, investigators concerned with the improvements of the governmental service must make some prior assumption about the desirability of such improvement. However, in making this assumption they inevitably sidestep the problem of the distribution of political power, since the ideal of improving the governmental service takes the given distribution of power for granted.[2]

The popular identification of bureaucracy with oppression cannot be taken lightly, since the extension of governmental functions has frequently curbed and

* This chapter is based on a longer article of the same title, published in *Public Administration Review*, V (Summer, 1945), 194–209. Material from this article is here reprinted with the permission of the Editor.

[1] For an analysis of the historical background of this ideology see the recent statement by Gunnar Myrdal, *An American Dilemma* (New York: Harper and Brothers, 1944), I, 432 ff.

[2] This corollary is not altered but rather confirmed if the administrative process is conceived of in terms of an arbitration of conflicting interests. In a sense all investigators concerned with the improvement of the governmental service conceive of administration in these terms. Cf. Avery Leiserson, *Administrative Regulation* (Chicago: University of Chicago Press, 1942), p. 14.

sometimes obliterated the freedom of the individual.[3] And although this extension has perhaps just as often led to the opposite result, there may today be additional reasons for the distrust of government, which finds emotional expression in the popular invectives against bureaucracy. Today, a revolutionary overthrow of government has become much more difficult than it was before the development of modern technology. Consequently the democratic right of revolution, of which Lincoln spoke, is now a right more in name than in fact.

Many of those, however, who distrust government do not think in terms of an ultimate recourse to revolution. Theirs is a more proximate concern with the neutrality of government administration. A literal interpretation of the democratic doctrine would have the people and their representatives determine the policies of their government. Administrators, then, have the task of putting these policies into effect. It is common knowledge, of course, that the customary accusations of bureaucracy and party politics which the "Outs" hurl against the executive branch of the "Ins" are but tools in the political struggle, which do not invalidate this ideal of administrative neutrality. But it is also well known that this struggle deeply affects the actual conduct of administrators in American society. It is the purpose of this study to elucidate some of the social factors which enhance or diminish the chance of American Federal administrators' being the neutral executors of legislative policies. In fact, the ideal of administrative neutrality itself may turn out to be a weapon in the constant struggle over a proper distribution and an equitable exercise of rights and obligations in our society. This study seeks to further an understanding of Federal administration by analyzing some of the factors which involve administrators in this struggle. Its underlying thesis is that no administrator can escape from this involvement. Its main purpose is to show this with regard to the social role of higher Federal administrators in the United States.

The contention that the administrator is not, and cannot become, the neutral executor of legislative enactments runs counter to widely-held beliefs. It conflicts with Max Weber's ideal-typical analysis and with both the liberal and the Marxian interpretation of bureaucracy. It is useful to state these differences at the outset. That statement will serve as a basis for a re-formulation of the problem of bureaucracy in the light of this question: What factors determine the role of the administrator in the struggle over the distribution and the exercise of power? There will follow in turn a brief outline of the major questions to which this study seeks to find answers.

[3] There is another aspect of the problem of bureaucracy and individual freedom which is not touched upon here. Both Karl Marx and Max Weber have emphasized with great persuasiveness that the division of labor under modern capitalism involves the separation of the worker in any field from his instruments of operation and generally the lack of meaningful participation of the individual in the processes of production and administration. From Marx, de Tocqueville, and Weber to Veblen and Mannheim this has been a recurrent theme, which has an important bearing on the problem of bureaucracy and freedom.

HISTORICAL BACKGROUND

The continuous expansion of the executive branch of government began with the rise of absolute monarchies in Europe. From the time of the Tudors it came to be recognized that the head of the state held an effective monopoly of power, in contrast to the feudal system, in which the power of government was delegated to semi-autonomous lords. Only the king could legitimately exercise physical coercion (within the bounds of certain customary rules and legal regulations).[4] The powers of the king were exercised by officials, whose duties became increasingly technical in character with the increasing complexity of governmental affairs. These officials, remunerated at first by favors from the king, came to receive regular salaries. Regular expenditures such as these required in turn the regularization of government revenues, which was guaranteed by a centrally organized system of taxation. Remuneration for government service was no longer identical with what the incumbent could get out of the office. Instead, salaries were paid by the treasury, and as a result remuneration became separated from the revenues received by the office. The struggle ever since the sixteenth century has been over the questions (1) how far, if at all, both the policies and the financing of government would be subject to the deliberations of a representative body; and (2) how representative of the people this lawgiving body would be. It is against this background that modern government administration arose. In order to understand it, we need to specify what we mean by administration and by bureaucracy.

ADMINISTRATION IN THE MODERN STATE

Administration in the modern state[5] is based on the principle that governmental policies are executed by appointed, technically qualified officials, who work full time and whose positions are related in terms of subordination and superordination. These officials exercise their functions according to learnable rules of procedure. Ideally, each position in the governmental hierarchy is characterized by specific, regular activities. Certain powers of command and coercion are ascribed to the position (not to the incumbent), and qualifications of the official are tested and consequently considered to be adequate for performing the duties of his office. The official is compensated for his services by a regular salary and by the expectation of a career-service carrying with it increasing grades of responsibility, salary advancement, pension provisions, security of tenure, and a certain social status. On the other hand, certain obligations or deprivations are associated with the office: the incumbent is bound to a faithful and impartial execution of the

---

4 Cf. Franklin Le Van Baumer, *The Early Tudor Theory of Kingship* (New Haven: Yale University Press, 1940).

5 The following characterization of bureaucracy follows closely the analysis of Max Weber. See H. H. Gerth and C. Wright Mills, *From Max Weber: Essays in Sociology* (New York: Oxford University Press, 1946), pp. 196–244. Cf. also Carl J. Friedrich, *Constitutional Government and Democracy* (Boston: Little, Brown and Co., 1941), ch. 2.

duties of office, and he cannot ordinarily expect a monetary compensation comparable to that of equivalent positions in private employment. The major characteristics of modern administration of the Western European type are based on the monopoly of legitimate coercion by the government, on a system of centralized taxation, on a body of qualified officials (working under the conditions outlined above), and on the supremacy of a nation-wide system of rational (that is, calculable) law.

The conclusions which may be drawn from the preceding ideal-typical characterization of modern government administration and its relation to the problem of power are threefold:

1. Administration in the modern state tends to operate like an automaton; that is, a body of officials whose performance of duty is professionalized and has consequently become independent of their personal sentiments and opinions.

2. As a result, policy is determined by the legislature, relayed to the executive branch, and executed at every step of the latter in optimum conformity with the original policy-decision.

3. Thus, whereas the exercise of authority is the lifeblood of administration the direction of its exercise is ideally determined outside the executive domain.

No actual administration conforms to this model. Yet, government administration in the countries of Western civilization do show many of these characteristics in varying degrees of approximation. It is Max Weber's contention that the social aspects of modern administration can best be studied if the historical causes of these approximations (or deviations) are ascertained. It is my belief that this procedure is not promising. It postulates for methodological reasons a model (or ideal type), whose basic assumption of administrative neutrality is derived from studies of the emergence of the modern state. The assumption is, in fact, a postulate which relates to the ideal of professional service and to the relative absence of corruption, personal vengeance, or favoritism in the modern governments of Western civilization.[6] It is not useful, however, to characterize modern administration by what distinguishes it from administration under feudalism. Rather, the traits of modern administration, as Weber has enumerated them, are in part contained in administrative rules and legislative enactments. For the rest these traits are the object of aspiration of some groups in modern society, notably the professional associations of civil servants and social reformers. It is, indeed, useful to understand the term "modern administration" in this sense.

[6] This idea was plausible in a society such as the German, in which political unification as well as the development of an industrial economy depended on government action. That action was successful only because a civil service had been created, whose loyalty to the service was unquestioning. As long as the government continued its pioneering role during the 18th and 19th centuries, this loyalty was easily mistaken for neutrality. Weber's reasons for this emphasis are also connected with his ideas concerning "rationalization," which refer to "greater rationality" in his discussion of bureaucracy, although they refer to "secularization" in other contexts. Cf. the writer's article "Max Weber's Interpretation of Conduct and History," *American Journal of Sociology*, LI (1945), 518–526.

The term "bureaucracy" should be reserved for a designation of all *informal relations* and *discretionary judgments*, by means of which administrators get their work done.   (This designation of bureaucracy applies regardless of whether either the formally stipulated rules of modern administration or the professional aspirations of modern administrators are thereby put into effect.)   Bureaucracy in this sense is the indispensable concomitant of any modern administration.

CONFLICTING THEORIES CONCERNING THE RELATION BETWEEN BUREAUCRACY AND THE EXERCISE OF POWER

The problem of administrative neutrality is of concern to all theorists who consider the forces that determine the exercise of governmental authority in modern society.   Outstanding among these are the liberal economists and the exponents of the Marxist tradition.   The former are predominantly concerned with the manner of, and the reasons for, the "interference of government with the market mechchanism."   The latter place major emphasis on the functions of government as an "executive committee of the ruling class."   Despite these conflicting interpretations of the role of government it is of interest that the theorists of both pursuasions hold essentially similar views of the role of administration in the exercise of power.   Their respective views of administration may be summarized as follows:

A. The Marxian view

1. Under capitalism, government administration is one of the instruments by means of which the bourgeoisie exercises its rule.

2. The recruitment of administrative personnel and the policies which it executes are both part of the political struggle, whose outcome is determined by the secular changes in the capitalist system of production.

3. The executive branch of government has, therefore, as much power as the ruling class delegates to it.   This "administrative arm of the ruling class" is a body of officials, which is so organized as to obey the policy directives which are handed down.   The formal regulations governing modern administration are designed to *guarantee* this relationship; whereas the informal, bureaucratic practices of administrators are the *means* by which the policies of the ruling class are carried out.

B. The *laissez-faire* view

1. Government authority is exercised in conformity with the commands of its directing officials.

2. The recruitment of administrative personnel and the policies which it executes are both part of the political process.   This process is the sum total of individual and group actions, concerned with the political promotion of self-interest. Whereas the parallel process in the economic sphere should be left to itself (within

an appropriate legal and political framework), in the political sphere it cannot be expected to operate in a similar fashion, since no "pricing-mechanism of power" exists. It is necessary, therefore, to convince the individuals in power that it is politically and economically imperative (for the preservation of freedom) to adopt such political measures as will safeguard free competition.

3. Such policies can be made effective as soon as the directing heads of governments are convinced. (This has so far not been successful because misled intellectuals and radicals have been the more influential.) Once these persons are convinced, however, liberal policies will be made effective, because the executive branch of the government has no power of its own (which could possibly be used to bring such policies to naught).

This summary may suffice to indicate that both views are in agreement on a number of points.[7] Both hold that the power of government in modern society is derived from forces outside the government, although one emphasizes the role of a powerful social class, and the other stresses the importance of powerful individuals as the real source of power.[8] Both theories interpret the role of administration as that of the "executive branch" with no power of its own. And both are finally agreed that the extension of administrative functions entails the diminution of individual freedom, although they differ basically about the causes and the nature of this development.

THE PROBLEM OF BUREAUCRACY RESTATED

It is important to restate the problem of bureaucracy in modern administration in the light of the foregoing discussion. For this purpose Weber's construction of the ideal type of administration serves as a convenient point of departure, since it presents us with a curious dilemma.

Weber noted that modern administration has become steadily more specialized. The importance of the skill element in modern administration is such, in his opinion, that power in the modern state cannot be exercised without professionally trained administrators, whatever the system of economic production. But he noted at the same time that this professionalization involved a code of ethics. Modern administration is, therefore, increasingly staffed by officials who will faithfully execute the duties of their office regardless of their personal disagreements with the policies involved. As a result, administrators are ready to serve whatever party is in power. In fact, the reliability of commercial transactions in

---

[7] For more extended treatment of these views cf. the author's "Bureaucracy and the Problem of Power," *Public Administration Review*, V (Summer, 1945), 197–204.

[8] In this sense many economic liberals believe that governmental power is derived from the interaction of diverse groups, analogous to the market in which interacting individuals determine the price. The powerful individuals are representatives of these groups. Cf. in connection with this doctrine J. S. Mill's statement that the "antagonism of influences is the only real security for continued progress." See his "Representative Government," in *Utilitarianism, Liberty and Representative Government* (London: E. P. Dutton and Co., 1910), 201.

an economy that has numerous government controls depends upon this neutrality of the civil service.[9] According to Weber, administrators are subservient to any ruling group, in so far as they adhere to the ideal of neutrality. They are discretionary in their exercise of authority, on the other hand, in so far as their skills are indispensable.

Weber observed also that modern governments are characterized by their exclusive authority to exercise physical coercion. Many factors will determine how this authority is exercised. But no executive can function if this authority is effectively challenged. Even if a government is overthrown, it will still be true that the insurgent group will claim the same authority and that it will depend on its own administration to put the new policies into effect.[10] It is, therefore, impossible to do without the type of administration which Weber holds to be characteristic of modern governments. Accordingly, there can only be changes among the groups that control the administrators. But any group can stay in power only so long as the position of its administration is secure. The effective authority of an administration is, therefore, an index of the power of government. Yet, the emphasis on neutrality and efficiency puts all considerations of policy affecting the exercise of authority outside the pale of administrative competence. Administrators are, therefore, vested with the exercise of authority, but incapable of determining in any way how the power of government should be used.

It is important to recognize that these tendencies in modern administration are mutually contradictory and that they exist simultaneously. There is a growth of administrative discretion in the sense that the administrator's freedom from supervision increases with the complexity of his skills. Professionalization of the civil service and the struggle over an administrative code of ethics have grown apace. The executive branch has acquired greater powers with the increase of its functions. And at the same time the legislature and the people insist on their right to determine policy and demand that the administrator should be neutral. It is not useful, however, to combine these tendencies through an ideal-typical construction. That procedure makes it difficult to discern the factors which account for the actual relations among administrative skills, professionalization, the growth of executive functions and of administrative discretion, and the demand

---

[9] Cf. Gerth and Mills, *op. cit.*, 219–220, for his analogy between governmental and judicial bureaucracy. In both cases he points out the *tendency* to "feed" laws or policies into the apparatus, which in turn issues decisions or executive rules in exact conformity with the directives. The reverse position is stated by Ludwig Bendix, *Gewisses und Ungewisses Recht* (Leipzig: W. Moeser Buchhandlung, 1930), pp. 46–54, where the identity between administration and adjudication is indicated by reference to the subjective element, which inescapably enters into both.

[10] Lenin maintained that the people would take over the government and that the existing state needed to be destroyed. He did not think this would result in chaos; the people themselves would exercise the functions of government, since these had become sufficiently simplified in capitalist society. Weber holds, on the other hand, that administration in the modern state has become more and more specialized, a tendency which would be enhanced by the advent of socialism. Administration by the people is, therefore, impossible, and destruction of the state would only result in chaos.

for neutrality.   In order to examine these relations it will be helpful to outline the principal variables that determine the exercise of authority in modern administration.

WHAT FACTORS DETERMINE THE EXERCISE OF AUTHORITY?

In modern administration high officials have a monopoly based on skill; they are irreplaceable because of their high technical qualifications which they must possess in order to fulfil the duties of their positions.[11]   In so far as these experts are irreplaceable they are able to sabotage policy directives or to put policies of their own into effect.   Whether they will use the power which their skills yield them depends in turn on the various factors that condition the exercise of administrative discretion.[12]   Among these factors the following are important:

a) Actual indispensability—a criterion which in itself involves a host of variables, such as irreplaceability of certain experiences or skill, which would ordinarily be a matter of time; urgency of the demand for the continuation of a specific public service; urgency of the demand for its continuation along lines peculiarly associated with the incumbent administrator[13]; ability of the incumbent to use personal influence and connections in support of his continued service.

b) The degree to which a code of professional ethics of civil servants has been developed.

c) The ease of alternative employments in other fields than government.

d) The unanimity of purpose in ranks of high civil servants (or the opposite attitude) with regard to the sabotage of opposed policies and/or a discretionary execution of desired policies.

e) Remoteness of administrative procedure from the individuals and groups who are affected.

f) The technical complexity of some executive actions, which by virtue of this complexity become matters of administrative discretion.

All these are intra-bureaucratic factors which help to determine the degree of administrative discretion.   They are in turn conditioned by forces which affect the executive branch from outside its hierarchical organization.   These forces

[11] Typically, this fact does not apply to government employees who are technical experts in the scientific or industrial fields.   For them substitutes can be found with relative ease, and they have characteristically low prestige in the civil service.

[12] Some of the factors under this heading are discussed by Otto Kirchheimer, "The Historical and Comparative Background of the Hatch Law," *Public Policy: A Yearbook of the Graduate School of Public Administration, Harvard University* II (1941), 341–373.

[13] This particular variant is, of course, in direct contradiction to the ideal of an efficient service, in which the personal equation is eliminated.   That it is not, is illustrated by the experience of the present military government in Germany, to cite but one example.   See also Ernst Fraenkel, *Military Occupation and the Rule of Law* (New York: Oxford University Press, 1944), pp. 25–37.

emanate from the socio-economic structure of society and affect the degree of administrative discretion in one or another of the ways indicated below:

a) Education and recruitment of the higher administrative personnel may create a group of administrators of similar social derivation and social philosophy. Under such circumstances there may exist an "extensive administrative autonomy," because both education and recruitment of the top administrators are such as to assure the legislature that the power of the executive will not be misused.[14]

b) The urgency of the demand for the continuation of public services.

c) The implicit or explicit demand for administrative discretion by various interest groups, in order to further their respective interests.[15] Such demands may be made:

(1) for the "socialization of risks", which requires discretionary action on the part of administrative agencies;[16]

(2) for the pursuit of a common enterprise, like war;

(3) for the promotion of cartelization, or conversely, for the freezing of given relationships among monopolistic enterprises.[17]

Such demands always involve at least the risk that the executive agency will go farther than desired, and in fact the fulfilment of these demands for executive action frequently make an extension of administrative discretion necessary. Ultimately, of course, the power which is actually in the hands of a bureaucracy may be tested by its own ability to stage a *coup d'etat* and by its ability and/or willingness to use the military apparatus of the government against external or internal threats to its position.[18]

Questions of this kind will have to be answered before the relation between the monopoly of skill and the growth of administrative discretion (monopoly of power) can be ascertained. The variables enumerated above raise doubts about the meaning of both terms. It is difficult to conceive of sellers of managerial skill who are strictly irreplaceable. Men possessing such skills are powerful, not because their skill makes them irreplaceable, but because, and to the degree that, their education and social derivation induce in them a common social philosophy.

[14] Cf. J. Donald Kingsley, *Representative Bureaucracy* (Yellow Springs: Antioch Press, 1944), pp. 261–283, for an analysis of the importance of this factor in English administration.

[15] Cf. for instance the demands of labor organizations during the war for more discretionary action on the part of the War Labor Board.

[16] Illustrations of this point may be found in the article by Fritz Karl Mann, "The Socialization of Risks," *Review of Politics*, VII (January, 1945) 43–57.

[17] A case in point is the problem of rate-differentials between different railroads before the Interstate Commerce Commission.

[18] Cf. the early analysis of the changing character of modern revolutions owing to changes in military technology in Friedrich Engels' introduction to Karl Marx, *The Class Struggle in France* (New York: International Publishers, 1934), pp. 1–30.

Administrative discretion is not a matter of skill but of independence from specific commands. That independence is derived from the authority which the organized representation of social groups[19] delegates to the administrator. Such delegation presupposes that administrative officials will faithfully execute policies of which they personally disapprove. But such impartiality can last only as long as there is a basic similarity of outlook between administrators and the forces shaping public policy. Without such agreement discretion would result in sabotage rather than in impartiality. Without it occasional or even frequent disagreements on policies would become politically and administratively unfeasible. It is, therefore, not true that administrators would serve everybody equally well.

This critique of the role which skill and neutrality play in modern administration should not divert our attention from the growth of discretion which has accompanied the development of executive functions. The true measure of this discretion may be gauged by the extent to which government, and especially its administrative agencies, remains uninfluenced by changes in class structure, by the shifting weight of social conflict groups, by long-run changes in public opinion, and ultimately by its ability to avert or withstand revolutionary upheaval.

THE PROBLEM OF AUTHORITY

The preceding discussion indicates that the popular identification of bureaucracy with an abuse of authority is misleading. By itself, administrative discretion is not evidence for such abuse. The question whether or not an exercise of discretion goes beyond the authority delegated to the administrator involves the whole problem of sovereignty, which cannot be discussed here. It may only be pointed out that recent theories either have conceived of law or the state as all-embracing metaphysical entities or have explained sovereignty away by some theory of pluralism. Most of these theories are little more than reflections of more basic postulates. Those, for instance, who regard modern capitalist society as moving inevitably in the direction of fascism will be inclined to state that sovereign authority is quickly disappearing,[20] and some writers profess the belief that under fascism the state has vanished altogether.[21] Others conceive sovereign authority to be derived in various ways from the organized expression of the popular will, because they are convinced that the conflicting group interests are ultimately reconcilable and that the administrator functions as the arbitrating agent. Finally, there are those who regard the basic documents of American

---

[19] The statement implies that authority is delegated by other representative bodies than the legislature. Implications of this statement are discussed in Chapter VIII below.

[20] Cf. Otto Kirchheimer, "In Quest of Sovereignty," *Journal of Politics* VI (May, 1944), 139–176.

[21] See Franz Neumann, *Behemoth* (New York: Oxford University Press, 1942), pp. 459–476.

government as the source of power and who consequently have no patience with any sociological or economic interpretation of the origin of authority.[22]

I allude to these large theoretical problems in order to indicate that theories of bureaucracy imply various philosophies of history.[23] These theories and philosophies make different estimates of the position which the administration of any country occupies between the extremes of anarchist decentralization and totalitarian centralization. That is to say, any government lies somewhere on the *continuum* between the type of political organization which has abandoned coercion in favor of free association and the type in which all authority and freedom are concentrated in a small group of men, whose orders are obeyed to the exclusion of individual deliberation. The student of bureaucracy, as here conceived, has the task of explaining the specific admixtures of compliance and initiative characteristic of the executive branches in different governments.[24] In this way he may contribute to an understanding of the factors which differentiate the respective positions of various modern governments on this *continuum* between anarchism and totalitarianism.

The use of this frame of reference may be illustrated as follows. One important aspect of bureaucracy is the accessibility of public employment. Max Weber thought that professionalization of the civil service had democratic implications, since it based that service on qualifications rather than birth. Yet the implications may just as easily be non-democratic, if such professionalization of the civil service is coupled with an authoritarian prestige in the eyes of the public.[25] How much social prestige does the official possess, and/or how much is public employment desired for the security of tenure, the prospects of regular advancement and the eventual pension? And conversely, how much is the civil service in disrepute precisely because of these attributes of employment in it?[26] In countries of similar economic structure like Great Britain and the United States these questions receive strikingly different answers. Further research may reveal that these different evaluations of public employment are coupled with different forms of obedience to authority and of public cooperation. It may be, therefore, that countries vary in the bureaucratic culture-patterns which affect the administrative exercise of authority. The following study seeks to advance our knowledge in

[22] Cf. Hyman E. Cohen, *Recent Theories of Sovereignty* (Chicago: University of Chicago Press, 1937), for a convenient summary.

[23] In speaking of philosophies of history I do not have in mind that these theories of bureaucracy are without empirical foundation. But they go beyond it by using predictions of future dvelopments as bases for the analysis of contemporary conditions.

[24] and [25] Both these points are discussed in greater detail in Chapter VII below.

[26] Cf. L. D. White, *The Prestige Value of Public Employment in Chicago* (Chicago: University of Chicago Press, 1929) and *Further Contributions to the Prestige Value of Public Employment* (Chicago: University of Chicago Press, 1931).

this respect about the social role of higher Federal administrators in the United States.

A critical problem of government today is the effect of bureaucracy on the manner in which the executive branch will exercise its power. It is assumed that in the foreseeable future government will have such power; but in this study the writer will not enter into the controversy over whether or not government should have this power. The preceding review of the literature has indicated that administration in a capitalist economy is never exclusively the initiator of the exercise of power, nor is it ever a neutral instrument in the hands of some directing group. The administrator plays a double role which compels him to comply with legislative rules and at the same time forces him to act on his own intiative whenever the contingencies of the administrative process call for it. Too great a compliance with statutory rules is popularly denounced as bureaucratic. Too great a reliance on initiative, in order to realize the spirit, if not the letter, of the law, is popularly denounced as an abuse of power, as interfering with legislative prerogative. Yet, government administration cannot do without either compliance or initiative. At its best it must seek to steer a course between the Scylla and Charybdis of both denunciations and the practices to which they refer.

In seeking to ascertain how administrators strike this balance, I have analyzed the social make-up and the working situations which characterize higher Federal administrators as a group and have attempted to find answers to the following questions:

(a) What is the social origin of higher Federal administrators?

(b) What is their educational background and how is its acquisition related both to their social origin and to their subsequent careers?

(c) What are the occupational career-lines of Federal administrators? Specifically, what light do they throw on the alternative incentives of private and public employment?

(d) Do the factors of social origin, education, and career-lines by themselves allow inferences as to the presence or absence of a common outlook among administrators?

(e) Is there a bureaucratic culture-pattern in the executive branch of the Federal government in the sense that certain pervasive pressures, emanating from Congress, the public, and the agency itself, affect the work of Federal administrators, regardless of their departmental specialization and the particular problems which it entails?

(f) If such a pattern exists, what are some of its characteristic consequences for the forms of administrative conduct?

Answers to these questions will not indicate the bearing of social origin on administrative decision-making.   That is the task of biographical research in combination with the analysis of specific administrative agencies.   On the other hand, answers to these questions will help to determine whether:

(a) Federal administrators in the United States constitute a cohesive social group in terms of the homogeneity or heterogeneity of their origin and career-patterns;

(b) the educational background of these administrators sets them apart as a distinct social group;

(c) public employment is below private employment both in social prestige and material reward;

(d) higher Federal administrators constitute a professional group united by an ethos of disinterested service to whichever political group is in power.

CHAPTER II

PROCEDURE OF THE STUDY

The preceding discussion has suggested that administrators have a better chance to exercise power in accordance with their own conviction (rather than in compliance with the legislative intent), if they are of one mind and if they constitute a homogeneous social group in terms of a common social background, education, and occupational experience. The existence of social homogeneity need not entail a common ideology, and a common ideology in turn does not necessitate an independent or arbitrary exercise of power. But if the members of a bureaucracy do not constitute a fairly cohesive group, one precondition of an independent exercise of power does not exist. If administrators do not form a cohesive social group, even a conscious attempt to contravene the legislative enactment would very likely be foiled, since the officials would work at cross purposes, each in turn desiring to see his policy realized.

PROBLEMS OF SAMPLING

Any person attempting to ascertain the degree of social homogeneity among American administrators is immediately confronted with the question from what population a representative sample may be drawn. In 1940 (the year chosen for this study in order to exclude, at any rate for purposes of sampling, wartime governmental personnel) Federal civilian employment (exclusive of national defense) was 836,492. It was desirable to select from this population a sample in which only those Federal employees would be included who were in positions high enough to affect policy formulation without being classed as political appointments. We are here concerned with the possible bearing of the social characteristics of administrators on the manner in which they will exercise their power. It is of major interest, therefore, to analyze the degree of social homogeneity that is characteristic of the group. This inquiry is preliminary since both the absence and the presence of social homogeneity would call for an investigation of factors other than that of social background[1] in order to account for the manner in which administrators of a given country exercise their power. Such preliminary inquiry is, nevertheless, indispensable, since it helps to clarify whether or not social background has a bearing on the problem at hand.[2] At the same time it was consistent with the emphasis on higher Federal officials, whose duties involved them in the process of policy formulation, to exclude from the sample all lower Federal per-

---

[1] For an enumeration of these other factors cf. Ch. I.

[2] For an example of a study in which a better understanding of administrators is obtained through the investigation of their social background, cf. Lysbeth Muncie, *The Junkers in German Administration* (Providence: Brown University Press, 1944).

sonnel.[3] Higher ranking officials were excluded whenever their work was of a predominantly technical character, which would affect policy formulation, if at all, only indirectly.[4]

The criteria of inclusion and exclusion may now be specified;

(a) Included were
1. Heads and assistant heads of large bureaus where the task is one of general direction rather than one requiring a specialist's competence;
2. Executive and administrative assistants;
3. Principal budget officials;
4. Principal personnel officers;
5. Directors of administrative divisions;
6. Regional and state officials of the Federal government having general responsibility in their respective areas;
7. Principal legal adviser of department or agency.

(b) Excluded were
1. Political heads and persons who hold posts requiring Senate confirmation or are concerned primarily with political problems;[5]
2. Bureau chiefs (including the chiefs of research bureaus) whose duties are dominated by specialist considerations;
3. Professional employees, such as engineers and doctors;
4. Army and Navy officers;
5. All except the principal budget and personnel officials;
6. All technical classes, such as accountants, auditors, purchasing agents, information specialists, and the like.

These criteria of selection may be criticized on a number of grounds. In the first place, the administrators who were selected in this way constitute an artificially delimited group. They are all administrative specialists who have in common the specific duties and qualifications which go with managerial work of high responsibility. But men who share these duties and qualifications in whatever degree have little else in common. Conversely, all large-scale organizations— public or private—require managerial work to effect their over-all administrative coordination. It follows that administrative specialists are engaged in all types of organizations and that administrative responsibility is virtually the only trait

[3] Federal personnel was classified as "lower" in any position carrying a salary of less than $4,000.

[4] The Official Register of the United States Government for 1940 was used as the basic source of information. For reasons of excluding from the sample groups of federal employees who merit independent consideration, the personnel of the Army and Navy were not considered in this study. I should like to acknowledge here the aid of Professors Leonard D. White and C. Herman Pritchett, both of the University of Chicago, in checking and rechecking the actual selection of names from the Official Register on the basis of the criteria set forth below.

[5] It is obviously difficult, if not impossible, to draw a line between political problems in the narrow sense (*i.e.*, affecting political parties) and policy problems, with which the administrator must deal whenever he brings a Congressional enactment nearer execution. However, some such crude distinction does exist, for instance, between the head of the NHA and its principal personnel officer.

which sets them off as a social group. Notwithstanding these reservations, it was thought useful to apply the criteria outlined above, because the administrative managers constitute a skill-group in modern governmental administration which is of importance because of the power whcih it exercises. It is true that they are frequently thought to be the neutral executors of policies which have been determined by others. They are ideally responsible for the execution, not for the formulation, of national policy. Yet in meeting this responsibility they are compelled to make political judgments, even if they are strict constructionists in matters of administrative neutrality. This is the case because policies are necessarily transformed in the process of execution. In fact, they are formulated in legislative enactments with a view to this transformation. The minor or major changes which interpretation of statute and adaptation to circumstance involve are matters of judgment in terms of administrative feasibility. Without contending in any way that the managers are the ruling class of today or at least tomorrow, as James Burnham has done,[6] we still maintain that the distribution of power in modern society is strongly affected by the spirit in which these judgments are made.

A second criticism of the criteria of sampling lies in the doubt that any clear distinction can be made between policy-making and administration. To study administrative managers as a group may for this reason be regarded as misleading, since a clear conclusion about their role as policy makers will be impossible to arrive at. The point is well taken, but it does not affect the sampling criteria in this instance. It is true that the complex interrelationships between policy formulation and the administrative process can be unravelled, if at all, only in the specific case, for which expert inside knowledge would be required. But the object here is not to analyze the interrelation in detail, but to probe the general setting of Federal administration which affects the manner in which policy is determined and executed. Such a study only aims at providing indispensable background material for case studies of this interrelationship.

A third criticism of the administrative managers (as selected by the foregoing criteria) would assert that this group is not representative of all the Federal officials who are concerned with policy. Thus Federal employees whose government work is predominantly of a technical character will nevertheless affect the policy which they help to execute. This criticism points to the difficulty of divorcing technical work from political and administrative considerations, and it is justified in this sense. It does not call into question the appropriateness of selecting

---

[6] James Burnham, *The Managerial Revolution* (New York: John Day, 1941), pp. 77–111.

[7] For instance, meteorologists in the Weather Bureau or chemists in the Food and Drug Administration. Other technicians are, on the other hand, concerned with policy. For this reason lawyers were not excluded from our sample. On their participation in policy formulation and execution, cf. the article by Fritz Morstein-Marx, "The Lawyer's Role in Public Administration," *Yale Law Journal*, LV (April, 1946), 498–526.

administrative managers for our sample. Rather it calls attention to the fact that this selection is necessarily arbitrary in leaving out whole groups of Federal employees whose inclusion would not seriously violate the criteria of selection. This has been done, nevertheless, for three reasons. First, there is some merit in the belief that the majority of Federal employees working in their technical capacity are only indirectly concerned with policy determination.[7] Second, men with technical training were not excluded from the sample if the position which they held in 1940 indicated that they were working at that time in an administrative capacity. Third, technical experts constitute a skill-group which is considerably different from administrators in terms of training and occupational experience and should, therefore, be considered separately.

METHODS OF THE STUDY

On the basis of the preceding considerations 428 names were selected from the Official Register for 1940. In view of the fact that the returns would be necessarily small there is some importance in the fact that these 428 administrators constituted—as nearly as it was possible to ascertain—the entire population of those who fitted the criteria of selection. Thus, although the returns would be small in absolute figures, they would still constitute a major part of the population from which they were drawn.[8]

The task of sampling was further complicated by the fact that the 428 names had to be proportionately distributed among all the government departments and agencies (with the exception of the Army and Navy). This was approximately assured in the original selection because in the larger departments there would obviously be more positions of the kind included in the sample than in the smaller agencies. But however good an approximation was achieved in the original selection, it should be emphasized that its representativeness is diminished by accidents of mailing and by a possible bias of the respondents, some of whom may have had a greater interest in a study of this sort than others. It is obviously difficult to assess this interest and its effect on the returns, but this shortcoming is

[8] All respondents included in the sample had either high CAF (clerical, administrative, fiscal) or high P (professional) classifications. It may be pertinent, therefore, to point out that in December, 1938 the CAF positions comprised 184,245, or 50.1 per cent, whereas the professional positions numbered 74,705, or 20.3 per cent, of all Classification Act positions. On the other hand, the positions paying $4,600 or over, which are predominantly CAF and P positions and from which the bulk of our sample was drawn, constitute only 14,958, or 4.1 per cent, of these positions. Moreover, the classified positions paying $5,600 or more numbered 5,911, or 1.6 per cent, of all Classification Act positions. These figures may serve to give a quantitative picture of the population from which our sample was drawn. It should be remembered, of course, that these figures only indicate the total number employed in CAF and P positions at the salary levels indicated. Consequently, the number of Federal employees in these categories who perform exclusively administrative duties would be very much smaller, thereby making our sample that much more representative. Although it is not possible to ascertain the total number of Federal employees corresponding to the criteria outlined above, it seems unlikely that they would number more than 2,000–3,000. For further details regarding Federal employment as a whole, including wartime developments, see "Salary Trends in Federal Employment," *Monthly Labor Review* (March, 1946), 1–16.

TABLE I

Distribution of Federal civilian employment (1940), number of names selected, number of questionnaires received, and number of cases for which only published biographical material was available listed by executive departments

Departments and independent offices	No. of civilian employees	No. of selected names	No. of returns*	Published biographies: No. of cases used
Executive Office	912	21	13	3
State Department	6,438	7	1	5
Treasury	60,200	27	12	2
Justice	17,769	10	3	1
Post Office	296,577	15	3	1
Interior	43,617	33	21	4
Agriculture	81,886	82	38	12
Commerce	25,288	34	13	3
Labor	3,653	27	16	3
Civil Aeronautics Authority	4,841	10	2	2
Civil Service Commission	3,980	5	3	0
Federal Communications Commission	1,081	4	1	2
Federal Deposit Insurance Corporation	1,850	4	1	0
Federal Loan Agency	18,472	28	5	3
Federal Power Commission	743	3	2	0
Federal Security Agency	29,146	36	21	4
Federal Trade Commission	650	6	1	1
Federal Works Agency	37,395	21	15	1
General Accounting Office	5,273	3	0	1
Interstate Commerce Commission	2,729	4	1	0
United States Maritime Commission	1,853	7	2	1
National Archives	380	3	1	1
National Labor Relations Board	763	4	2	1
National Railroad Adjustment Board	84	1	0	0
Railroad Retirement Board	2,248	7	3	1
Securities and Exchange Commission	1,611	9	4	3
Tariff Commission	290	3	0	1
Tennessee Valley Authority	18,320	5	3	0
Veterans' Administration	41,383	8	4	1
Total		428	192	56

* This column combines the number of returns from the original (160) with those from the supplementary questionnaire (32).

perhaps alleviated by the observation of the writer that interest in problems of administration is very widespread in Washington, regardless of one's educational background.[9]

[9] In discussing the problems of sampling involved in this study Mr. Calvin Dedrick of the U. S. Census Bureau stressed particularly the danger of obtaining an over-representation of administrators with advanced educational

Questionnaires were sent to the 428 persons at their government addresses, and after an interval of four weeks a follow-up letter was sent to those from whom no answer had been received. A total of 160 questionnaires was returned. In an attempt to augment this return various Biographical Directories were examined for sketches of the men and women whose names appeared in the original list of 428. A new letter was sent to all for whom published biographical data could be found. This included a one-page, abbreviated questionnaire which, in addition to the published data, was found in most cases to be sufficient to make these returns comparable to the full-questionnaire returns. A total of thirty-two returns was thus received, bringing the total returns for the whole study to 192 out of 428.[10]

As was to be expected, many of the persons for whom published biographical sketches were found, failed to answer the second, shortened questionnaire as well. Wherever possible (especially with regard to educational background, occupational career, and club membership) this material was used, nevertheless, to augment the sample of 192, in this way bringing the total number of cases up to 248.[11]

INTERVIEWS

In addition to the sample-study outlined above the writer had the opportunity of interviewing twenty-eight administrators (or persons with previous administrative experience) in their offices in Washington, D. C., or in their present business offices.[12]

The persons interviewed were selected with a view to their long acquaintance with the Federal government and their various and divergent positions in it.

---

background. Among the returns received, on the other hand, the proportion coming from men with only high-school or partial college (or business school) education was considerable, although its representativeness is difficult to judge. It should be borne in mind, however, that the administrators with little educational background are almost invariably the older men, whose proportion among higher administrators is obviously smaller (because of the age factor) and whose interest in problems of public administration after a lifetime of service is naturally keen. Thus, the risk of having an under-representation of administrators with little educational background is, at any rate, diminished. At present, however, we cannot estimate the representativeness of our sample in this respect. Table I indicates that old-line departments and agencies are under-represented, although their personnel figures are inconclusive as a basis of sampling administrative managers.

[10] See Table I for a tabulation of the number of returns by agencies, contrasted with the number of names originally selected from these agencies. Samples of the questionnaires and the various accompanying letters are included in the Appendix.

[11] It is recognized, of course, that in using material from *Who's Who*, *Current Biography*, and similar sources one must make allowances for the editorial policy of these publications, which determined the selection of persons to be included. However, in this instance it should be remembered that the names were taken from our original list, which was drawn up independently. The thirty-two cases, for whom complete data were obtained in the manner indicated above, were in fact a corrective in the sense that disproportionately many of the well-publicized people failed to answer the first letter. Consequently, it is permissible to treat the first and second returns as a unit, whereas the fifty-six additional cases, for which only published sources were available, do tend to over-represent the nationally prominent figures contained in the original list. It will be seen from this description of the sources for our data that the totals will be different in many instances.

[12] The selection of the persons to be interviewed was made with the aid of Professors Leonard D. White and Louis Wirth of the University of Chicago.

Table I-A shows the agencies with which they were associated at the time of the interview.

Of the interviewees listed as at present in private employment two had received and answered the questionnaire. (None of the other persons interviewed had been included in the sample.) Another three persons, who were privately employed, were at the time of the interview associated with such agencies as the Brookings Institution and the Public Administration Clearing House after long experience in the Federal government.

TABLE I-A

Number of persons interviewed, listed according to government agency or business in which they are employed

Employed by	No. of persons
Office of Price Administration	2
State Department	1
Social Security Board	2
Civil Service Commission	2
Bureau of the Budget	6
Commerce Department	1
Federal Security Agency	1
National Housing Administration	2
Council of Personnel Administration	1
Bureau of the Census	1
Treasury	1
Congress*	2
Private Employment	6

* This item refers to one Congressman and to an employee of another Congressman.

The plan of the interview was to proceed in as informal a manner as possible. The writer, after presenting his letter of introduction, gave a very brief sketch of the questionnaire study. In addition he indicated that he was interested in learning about the informal working conditions of the higher Federal service, rather than the formal procedures of the administrative process. Did the working experience of the person interviewed suggest any insights or particular examples pertinent to this idea? All interviewees (except one) responded to this approach readily. In view of the exploratory character of this part of the study it was thought desirable to introduce as few preconceived ideas into the interviews as possible. (The only exceptions to this were a few instances in which the person interviewed commented first on some aspect of the questionnaire study, before addressing himself to the informal aspects of administration.)

The comments of each person were put down during the interview by way of key phrases suggesting the major problems touched upon. Immediately after the interview these were expanded into full-length paragraphs on each of the points discussed. This material was expanded still further about ten days later and then laid aside. After an interval of a month and a half, during which the questionnaire study was written up, the writer re-read each of the interviews, noting the major problem areas on which each of them touched. This material was then compared with such references to informal aspects of the administrative process as could be found in the literature, and, thus enhanced, it was written up in terms of the three aspects of the bureaucratic culture-pattern on which the material seemed to warrant extended analysis. This is contained in Chapter VIII of the present study.

CHAPTER III

THE SOCIAL ORIGIN OF HIGHER FEDERAL ADMINISTRATORS

AGE-COMPOSITION AND PLACE OF BIRTH

The criteria of sampling set forth above have emphasized the higher brackets of the Federal service. Consequently, the age distribution of the respondents is skewed in favor of the 40–54 age-group; younger men have not had so much chance to rise in the government service, and the number of older men is diminished by deaths. It is important to compare the age-distribution of the sample with the age-distribution of professional and administrative personnel in the Federal government as a whole.

The comparison with the professional and administrative service as a whole is reassuring. It confirms the effectiveness with which our critieria of selection were applied. On the whole the higher administrators can be expected to be an older group; this is borne out by a comparison of the age distribution of the sample with that of the entire professional and administrative personnel. If selection of names with no knowledge of age results in a distribution which is proportionately lower in the age-group up to 39 but higher above 40, we have additional evidence that the sample group is reasonably well selected.

The group is predominantly rural and small-town in origin, as indicated in the following tables. The 1900 census was used to ascertain the size of towns which the respondents indicated as their place of birth, since a majority were born around the turn of the century. In 24 additional cases the names of the towns which had been indicated on the questionnaire could not be found in the 1900 census, either because these places were listed as rural in the census or because the towns changed their names. Eleven other respondents were foreign-born and were not included in the foregoing tabulation, although 6 out of 11 indicated small towns as their places of birth. (In the remainder of the cases the places of birth were not given.)

These data are inconclusive as long as no data on the migration of comparable occupational groups exist. Taussig's study of American business leaders[1] does contain such comparable data. His data indicate that higher Federal administrators are predominantly of small-town origin in contrast to business leaders. Of the latter only 2.6 per cent came from localities with less than 2,500 population, as against 41.4 per cent of the administrators. On the other hand, 63.9 per cent of the business leaders, but only 26.8 per cent of the administrators, were born in cities of 100,000 and over. In the light of both the fact that our sample of administrators represents a younger group than the business leaders sampled by Taussig

---

[1] F. W. Taussig and C. S. Joslyn, *American Business Leaders* (New York: The Macmillan Co., 1932), p. 44.

and the fact that for the nation as a whole the urban population exceeded the 50.0 per cent mark only in 1920, the small-town origin of Federal administrators

TABLE II

Number and per cent of respondents listed by 5-year age-groups in 1940 as compared with the percentage distribution of Federal employees in the professional and managerial occupations (December, 1938)*

Age group	Respondents in 1940		Federal employees (1938) in %	
	Number	Per cent	Professional	Managerial & administrative
30–34	18	7.5	21.7	15.1
35–39	21	9.0	17.1	16.0
40–44	52	22.0	18.0	20.9
45–49	42	18.0	16.7	18.1
50–59	73	31.5	19.7	21.3
60 years and over	28	12.0	6.8	8.6
Total..........	234	100.0	100.0	100.0

* The age breakdown for Federal employees in professional and managerial occupations was recalculated from M. L. Smith and K. R. Wright, "Occupations and Salaries in Federal Employment," *Monthly Labor Review* (January, 1941), p. 72, Table 3.

TABLE III

Number of respondents listed by size of population of their places of birth in 1900

Size of place of birth	Number of respondents	Per cen
Below 2,500	85*	41.4
2,500–4,999	16	7.8
5,000–9,999	11	5.4
10,000–24,999	16	7.8
25,000–49,999	11	5.4
50,000–99,999	11	5.4
100,000–499,999	25	12.2
500,000 and over	30	14.6
Total.................................	205	100.0

* This figure includes 10 cases in which only the counties were named, but not the localities in which the respondent was born.

when compared with that of prominent businessmen is indeed, conspicuous. In this context it is also of interest to mention that according to a study of an entirely different group of government personnel (Foreign Service) the majority come from the run-of-the-mill small town.[2]

TABLE IV

Number and per cent of respondents listed according to state of origin

State	No. of respondents born in the state	Percentage distribution	Rank order of states, 1940 population
New York	19	8.3	1
Massachusetts	16	6.9	8
Illinois	15	6.5	3
Missouri	15	6.5	10
Iowa	15	6.5	20
Kentucky	11	4.8	16
Pennsylvania	10	4.3	2
Ohio	10	4.3	4
New Jersey	9	3.9	9
D. C.	9	3.9	37
Virginia	8	3.4	19
Minnesota	7	3.0	18
Kansas	7	3.0	29
Indiana	6	2.6	12
Tennessee	6	2.6	15
Maryland	6	2.6	28
Michigan	5	2.1	7
Wisconsin	5	2.1	13
South Carolina	5	2.1	25
Nebraska	5	2.1	32
North Carolina	4	1.7	11
Georgia	4	1.7	14
Colorado	4	1.7	33
Vermont	4	1.7	46

* The states having three respondents each were California, Texas, Alabama, and South Dakota. The states having two respondents each were Louisiana, Mississippi, West Virginia, Washington, and Utah. The states having one respondent each were Florida, Connecticut, Maine, Rhode Island, Delware, New Hampshire, and Wyoming. None of the respondents came from any of the remaining states.

In connection with this brief survey of the rural-versus-urban derivation of higher administrators, their distribution by states of origin was also tabulated (Table IV). There is, however, little value in a compilation of this sort. For

[2] According to Frank Roudybush, through whose courtesy the writer was able to compare the material of this study on some points with similar unpublished data on the personnel of the Foreign Service and the State Department. Of this sample of 767 Foreign Service Officers 53.2 per cent came from towns of up to 50,000 population as against 67.8 per cent in our sample. The difference is, however, considerably exaggerated owing to the fact that Roudybush used 1940 population figures, whereas the tabulation above is taken from the 1900 census.

purposes of approximating a proportional representation of states in Federal employment, current legal residence rather than state of origin is usually considered.[3] This interest in the question of proportional distribution of appointments has obvious political implications, which will not be considered here. Yet for a study of the social composition of higher Federal administrators it would be far more important to obtain a breakdown by employment status (or by salary brackets) for the geographical distribution of the Federal service, preferably for different types of government agencies. The small size of our sample did not make this part of our inquiry feasible.[4] There is reason to believe, however, that the higher Federal personnel of the different government agencies is not selected either at random on the basis of qualification alone or proportionately, but rather from the geographic regions and/or the specific interest groups with which the respective hiring agency is predominantly concerned.

SOCIAL ENVIRONMENT

Apart from the rural and small-town origin of 139 out of 205 administrators, it is important to ascertain whether their social derivation indicates any preponderance of one group as against others. The literature on the problem of occupational transmission is very sketchy and no over-all picture of social mobility in America is available. Previous studies, such as that by Anderson and Davidson,[5] indicate that the mobility of successive generations occurs between adjacent levels of the occupational hierarchy, and they confirm, of course, the familiar shift away from agriculture towards trade and the professions.

The data on social origin, which were obtained in this study, are of similar interest, although their value is impaired by the small number of returns (180) on this particular item. In order to insure rough comparability in a field in which as yet no standardized occupational classification exists, it was thought advisable to adopt a modification of the old census classification, although its many defects are recognized.[6]

This distribution of the occupational origin of higher Federal administrators may be readily compared with a similar distribution of American business leaders obtained by Taussig, which has been added in the right-hand column of Table V.

[3] Cf. for a discussion of data on geographic distribution of appointments and an emphasis of their unreliability Kenneth C. Vipond, "Memorandum as to Apportionment of Appointments in Washington, D. C.," in U. S. Committee on Civil Service Improvement, *Documents and Reports to Accompany Report on Civil Service Improvement* (Washington: Government Printing Office, 1942), III, Part 1, 133–142.

[4] Some data on this point were, however, obtained through interviews and are discussed below.

[5] H. D. Anderson and P. E. Davidson, *Occupational Mobility in an American Community* (Stanford: Stanford University Press, 1937).

[6] In this respect I have followed previous studies in this field, such as the one by Taussig and Joslyn or by Anderson and Davidson already referred to. See also for valuable material Walter J. Greenleaf, *Economic Status of College Alumni* (Bulletin 1937, No. 10 of the U. S. Office of Education; Washington: Government Printing Office, 1939) and F. C. Babcock, *The U. S. College Graduate* (New York: Time, Inc., 1940).

Allowance should be made for the fact that Taussig does not list the farmer, who is also engaged in business, in a separate category. Even so it is quite plain that the administrators are significantly more rural in origin than the business leaders. Moreover, a considerably larger proportion of administrators comes from professional families rather than from families engaged in large-scale business, whereas this relation is reversed in the case of business leaders. This contrast is even enhanced, if it is remembered that Taussig's study was undertaken in 1928, when

TABLE V

Distribution of 180 respondents by father's occupation

Father's occupation	Number	Per cent	Taussig's distribution in %*
Laborer (unskilled or semi-skilled)....................	2	1.1	2.2
Skilled laborer (or mechanic).........................	16	8.9	8.6
Clerk or salesman....................................	6	3.3	5.0
Farmer			
a. Owner...	38	21.1⎫	12.4
b. Owner and businessmanª......................	14	7.9⎭	
Small businessman..................................	34	18.9	26.1
Large businessman..................................	13	7.2	30.6
Government service.................................	6	3.3	1.7ᵇ
Professional.......................................	51	28.3	13.4
Total...	180	100.0	100.0

* The figures in this column are taken from Taussig and Joslyn's *American Business Leaders* (New York: The Macmillan Co., 1932) and are here reprinted by permission of the publisher.

ª This category refers to farmers who are also engaged in business.

ᵇ In Taussig's tabulation 1.7 per cent are listed under "other occupations," of which government service was only a part. (See Taussig and Joslyn, *op. cit.*, p. 82.)

opportunities for occupational advancement had presumably been greater than in the 1930's.

In evaluating the data presented above, one should observe caution in two respects. In the first place, by lumping together the social origin of both young and old administrators we fail to bring out whether or not their origin has changed over a period of time. Thus it is important to know, for instance, whether the proportion of men who went into government service from professional families has always been around 28 per cent. Our data are, of course, insufficient to answer this question fully. But they seem indicative of the major trends characteristic of the families of farmers, small businessmen, and professionals,[7] if they are

[7] The other occupational categories are omitted in the following tabulation, because the corresponding number of cases is too small to make percentage calculation meaningful.

tabulated by the major age-groups of the respondents. These data show that fewer of the young and more of the old administrators come from farmer's families, whereas more of the young but fewer of the old officials come from professional families. Moreover, the discrepancy in social origin between young and old is greater in the case of farmers' families, whereas it is smaller among the professionals. This not only confirms the shift away from agriculture, but it indicates

TABLE VI

Per cent age-distribution of respondents listed by father's occupation

Father's occupation	No.	Age of respondent			
		30–39	40–49	50–59	60 and over*
Farmer..................................	52	6.4	16.8	29.6	41.1
Small businessman	34	22.5	22.0	11.1	23.5
Professional..............................	51	38.7	27.2	25.9	23.5

* Because of the very much smaller number of cases in this age-category the percentage figures under it must be discounted.

TABLE VII

Per cent age-distribution of American business leaders listed by selected father's occupations

Father's occupation	Age of respondent*			
	30–39	40–49	50–59	60–69
Farmer...........................	4.8	9.2	13.4	18.5
Minor executive................... Owner of small business............	26.5	27.1	27.7	27.2
Professional......................	12.2	12.3	12.7	14.3

* Taussig's data are computed for 5-year age-groups. The above figures were arrived at by halving the difference between the two 5-year age-groups in each instance. The distortion incurred thereby does not exceed one per cent.

that the percentage of administrators coming from professional families has always been rather high.[8] A comparison of these data with those compiled by Taussig in his study of American business leaders[9] helps to underscore these points. Limited though such data are, they do suggest that the civil service provides opportunities for upward social mobility to persons whose background bars them from such mobility by way of a business career.

Business leaders as well as administrators have in the past come more frequently

[8] The data on small-business families in the following Table VI seem to be inconclusive, although they suggest perhaps that the proportion of administrators coming from such families has remained fairly stable over the years.
[9] Taussig, *op. cit.*, p. 98.

from farmer's families than in more recent years, although in this instance the decline of administrators is more noticeable, for the obvious reason that occupational advancement by way of government service has all along been more accessible to farmers than by way of large-scale business. Roughly the same proportion of business leaders and administrators have come from families of small businessmen, and this proportion has remained relatively stable. On the other hand, business leaders and administrators of professional origin differ considerably, the proportion of the former being relatively small and stable, while the proportion of the latter has been significant and increasing.[10]

A second caution about these data on social origin is perhaps more important. To ascertain the occupation of a person's father is not in itself very revealing. It hardly reveals the significance of this fact for his own occupational career beyond a minimal indication of his early environment. This is especially true when the occupational categories used are so broad as to indicate very little with regard to the help a person may have received from his family upon the launching of his career. In view of these reservations it is useful to characterize somewhat further the social environment from which this group of administrators has come by tabulating in parallel columns the occupational status of fathers, fathers-in-law, and brothers. In a fourth column the principal occupations of the respondents has been added. Many of them had had prolonged careers in other fields before entering the government service. It is, therefore, important to note their principal occupations; that is, that occupation in which by 1940 they had spent the largest number of years since the inception of their working lives, whether that had been within the Federal government or outside. This, of course, accounts for the fact that the respondents are not all listed under "Government Service." (For purposes of contrast the percentage distribution by occupational classes of the gainfully employed male population in 1900 has also been added.)

These figures give a number of interesting insights into the social environment of the group as a whole. A tendency is noticeable for men in the group to choose wives coming from families which are somewhat higher up in the occupational hierarchy. Thus, among the fathers-in-law there are fewer laborers and farmers than among the fathers of the respondents, but more professionals and large businessmen. If this is characteristic of the group as a whole, trial cross-tabulations show that a considerable proportion of the cases fall within the same or adjacent occupational categories. That is to say, of all the cases sampled, a little more than 25 per cent married into families of their own occupational level; that is, sons of farmers married farmer's daughters, sons of professionals married daughters of professionals, and so on. These tabulations also show that upward

---

[10] It should be borne in mind that this comparison between Taussig's data and ours is only suggestive, since the discrepancy between the number of cases in the two studies is very great.

TABLE VIII

Per cent distribution listed by occupations of the gainfully employed male population (1900), of fathers, fathers-in-law, brothers,* and respondents

Occupation	Gainfully employed males	Fathers	Fathers-in-law	Brothers	Respondents
Laborer (unskilled or semi-skilled).	39.0	1.1	—	0.4	—
Skilled laborer (or mechanic)......	14.0	8.9	4.9	7.8	—
Clerk or salesman...............	6.1	3.3	4.0	6.4	1.7
Farmer......................	25.3	29.0	16.3	9.2	1.2
Small businessman...............	6.6ª	18.9	19.5	14.7	2.9
Large businessman...............	1.7ᵇ	7.2	16.3	17.0	5.0
Government service..............	3.6ᶜ	3.3	2.4	7.8	58.5
Professional....................	3.2	28.3	36.6	36.7	30.7
Total......................	100.0	100.0	100.0	100.0	100.0

* In cases where more than one brother was listed, the occupation of each was added in the appropriate occupational category.

ª This item includes the census classifications of "minor executive" and "owner, small business."

ᵇ This item includes the census classifications of "major executive" and "owner, large business."

ᶜ This item covers more than "government service" in the census classifications. It is listed there under "others," including a number of miscellaneous occupations which are grouped together with government service.

TABLE IX

Per cent distribution of American and German administrators listed by their fathers' occupations

Occupation of father	American administra- tors—%	German administra- tors—%*
Laborer (unskilled or semi-skilled)............................	1.1	0.4
Skilled laborer (or mechanic)...............................	8.9	4.1
Clerk, salesman }ª Small and large business	29.4	25.0
Farmer...	29.0	14.9
Profession (including teachers, judges, and clergymen)ᵇ...........	28.3	20.5
Government service..................................	3.3	32.1
Unclassified.......................................	—	3.0

* These data are taken from the study of Otto Most, "Zur Wirtschafts und Sozialstatistik der hoeheren Beamten in Preussen," *Schmoller's Jahrbuch*, XXXIX (1915), 214.

ª The figures for this category are not comparable, since under it too many different occupations are included. The German study does not have a breakdown comparable to the one used here.

ᵇ This parenthesis is explained by the fact that teachers, judges, and clergymen are government employees in Germany and are listed as such in all official statistics.

movement in the occupational ladder occurred between adjacent levels in a large number of cases, as far as intermarriage was concerned.[11] Thus, 45.2 per cent of the sons of farmers married daughters of farmers and of small businessmen; 56.4 per cent of the sons of small businessmen married daughters of farmers and of small businessmen. Of the sons of large business families, 31 per cent married within their own social group, while about 45 per cent married the daughters of professionals. (On the other hand, almost two-fifths of the daughters of professionals were married to sons of the first five occupational categories; that is, at levels not adjacent to that of their families.) These data certainly support the view that intermarriage did play in some measure the role of facilitating upward occupational mobility.

A comparison of the occupational distribution of fathers and brothers shows roughly the same tendencies as the figures on the intermarriage of respondents, except that these tendencies are considerably enhanced. Movement away from farming is more striking among the brothers, and the tendency is to go into selling, large business, government service, and the professions. But the stronger tendency to rise by way of occupational advancement rather than marriage is also evident. Comparable cross-tabulations show that only 30 per cent of the sons of farmers stay in farming or small business (but 45 per cent married within these groups); 17 per cent of the farmers' sons go into large business, and 31 per cent go into the professions. Of the sons of small businessmen about 20 per cent stay in their fathers' occupations (but 39 per cent marry the daughters of small businessmen); 28 per cent go into large business and 35 per cent go into the professions (although only 21 per cent marry the daughters of professionals). Here again it was true for the group as a whole that about 25 per cent of the brothers stayed in their fathers' occupations.

More striking than either of the preceding comparisons is, of course, the contrast between the occupational distribution of brothers and respondents. Movement away from skilled labor, farming, and small business has led either into government work or the professions, and the high representation of professionals in this group of Federal administrators would indicate that professional work and civil service have become in large measure interchangeable for them. It is certainly true to say for the group as a whole that public employment and professional work have functioned as avenues of advance which were alternative not only to farming but to business.

It is useful to cite in this context the only comparable study of higher government administrators which has come to my attention. This is a study of the salaries and the social origin of a sample of higher German administrators which was conducted prior to World War I. At this point it is of primary interest to compare the social origin of administrators in the two countries.

---

[11] And in so far as the crude occupational classification can catch status differentials.

It should be emphasized, of course, that such a comparison cannot be accurate in any literal sense, since the occupational categories in use in the two countries differ a great deal.   But the comparison is indeed useful, if it is understood as indicating the orders of magnitude involved.   The most striking difference lies in the degree to which German administrators were recruited from families of administrators as against the Americans, for whom this source played a negligible role. This contrast is heightened if the German judges, teachers, and clergymen are counted, not as professionals, but as government employees; accordingly, 48.5 per cent of the German administrators come from families already in the employ of the government.[12]

The preceding data on the social environment of one sample of higher Federal administrators do not contain a definitive answer to the question to what extent the father's occupation aids or hinders the son's (or daughter's)[13] career.   The data presented so far do show that the group comes from families in which the movement away from farming into business, and particularly into the professions and government service, is pronounced.   By far the most important avenue through which this mobility is accomplished is education, and our educational data throw some light on the question how important family background is for the occupational career of the group.

[12] The exact breakdown is as follows: 11.2 per cent of the sample came from families in the lower and middle bracket of the civil service; 20.9 per cent came from families in the higher civil service; and 16.4 per cent came from families of teachers, judges, and clergymen.

[13] In view of the small number of women represented in the sample they were not tabulated separately.

CHAPTER IV

THE EDUCATION OF HIGHER FEDERAL ADMINISTRATORS

SOCIAL ORIGIN AND EDUCATIONAL BACKGROUND

This sampling of Federal administrators indicates that a large proportion have had a college education or have done graduate work. Out of the sample of 242 administrators 16, or 6.6 per cent, finished only high school. Another 83, or 34.6 per cent, went to college; but out of these 31, or 13.2 per cent, did not finish college, whereas the remainder of 52, or 21.4 per cent, graduated. As against these 99, who went to high school or college, 143, or 59 per cent, did graduate work, and out of these 134 received higher degrees. It may be noted that these 134 collectively earned 185 higher degrees.[1]

These data indicate that higher Federal administrators are a well-educated group. Again allowance should be made as to the representativeness of the sample, both in terms of its original selection and in terms of the greater interest of some administrators in cooperating with a study of this sort.[2]

Additional evidence indicates, nevertheless, that our sample is representative of the higher Federal service. The writer has had an opportunity to see the results of a similar but unpublished study of one of the highly professionalized bureaus of the Federal government.[3] The study covered the entire bureau and consequently included its clerical personnel. Of the bureau's personnel almost the same proportion as in our sample had done graduate work and exactly the same proportion had earned higher degrees. This fact would seem to indicate that the sample of this study does not over-represent the professional administrator. Caution, however, is still advisable, because the sample may not be representative enough of the old-line agencies. This possibility is suggested both by the under-representation of some old-line agencies in our sample (for example, the State, Justice, and Post Office Departments) and by the relatively professional character of the bureau with which the foregoing comparison was made.

[1] A comparison of these data with those provided by Mr. Roudybush (Letter of July 22, 1946 to the writer) on a sample of Foreign Service Officers brings out the significance of education among higher Federal administrators. Out of a total of 676 Foreign Service Officers 4.9 per cent went only to high school, 19.4 per cent went to college but did not graduate, 56.3 per cent obtained a Bachelor's degree, whereas another 19.4 per cent received higher (M. A. or Ph. D.) degrees.

[2] In the writer's estimation, the second of these is not a serious limitation. Interest in studies such as this seems to be widespread regardless of educational background, since all administrators not only create bureaucratic problems but suffer from them. On the whole I have the impression that the failure to answer was fairly random; in many instances letters of apology were received, indicating lack of time as the reason why the request for answering the questionnaire could not be granted. However, the Post Office may be an exception in this respect.

[3] Although I am not at liberty to identify the bureau, it may be of interest to add that, whereas 7.7 per cent had P and 87.3 per cent had CAF classifications, 42.1 per cent of the bureau's personnel received an annual salary in excess of $4,600. Thus the number of high CAF's is considerable.

In the previous section the occupational distribution of the fathers of the group indicated their home environment in broad terms. Such data cannot furnish an answer to the question of how much his home environment helped or hindered a person's career.[4] Part of this answer may be found in a breakdown of the educational data. In this connection it should be remembered that educational opportunities in this country have vastly increased since the turn of the century. A higher evaluation of education has been both cause and consequence of this development. As a result the relation between age and educational background from the sample group is worth noting (Table X).

TABLE X

Per cent distribution of respondents listed by age-groups and highest level of education achieved

Top–level of education	Age of respondents		
	30–39	40–49	50–70
High school (non-graduates and graduates).......................	—	3.0	12.6
College non-graduates (including evening and business school).......	9.7	20.4	18.5
College graduates...	9.7	20.4	15.6
Graduate work (without degree)................................	2.4	3.0	4.8
Higher degrees...	78.2	53.2	48.5
Total..	100.0	100.0	100.0

Among the older groups the proportion of administrators who did not go farther than high school, or who did not complete their college education, is greater. It is noticeable, on the other hand, how many of them did go on to graduate work. But while the difference in age in the aggregate affects the amount of educational experience, it does not seem to have an important bearing on the question whether or not this education was obtained before or after the person entered upon his career. The inference seems justified that family assistance was forthcoming in all instances in which a person had an opportunity to complete his education before beginning his occupational career. It would seem to be true, on the other hand, that a person was earning at least part of his educational expenses whenever the period of his educational training overlapped that of his career. In this case the inference seems justified that the family was at the time unable to meet his

---

[4] It is sometimes suggested that such an answer can be provided only if information is obtained on the earnings of the father at the time of a person's high-school training. Such data, however, are likely to be very unreliable and, even if reliable, very difficult to evaluate. Another difficulty which this suggestion is designed to overcome is the questionable reliability of information on the father's occupation. This difficulty is a real one, although the suggestion hardly helps to alleviate it. On the whole reliance must be placed on the informant's subjective categorization

educational expenses and that he had to begin earning a living before his education could be completed.[5]

In view of these considerations it is interesting to observe what proportion of each age-group completed their education before or after entry upon their careers (Table XI).

The percentages shown for the 50-and-over age-group are only apparently out of line in view of the fact that 12 per cent of those within this age-group who completed their education before entering upon their career went only to high school. Even if the predominance of high-school education in earlier days is taken into account, it would still be true that the parental financing of high-school education is not comparable to the financing of college or graduate study. If, on the other hand, these 12 per cent who went only as far as high school are excluded,

TABLE XI

Proportion of respondents completing their education before and after entry upon career, listed by age-groups

Age-group of respondents	Education completed	
	Before	After
	Entry upon career	
30–39	53%	47%
40–49	53%	47%
50 and over	63%	37%

the result is that 57 per cent of this age group completed their education before, whereas 43 per cent completed their education after entry upon a career. These results are only suggestive because of the small size of the sample. Yet the stability of these proportions regardless of age is remarkable. Over the years in roughly half of the cases the occupational success, in so far as it depended on education, was the result of the person's own efforts. In the other half of the cases that success was in varying degrees aided by parents.[6]

[5] It is possible, of course, to imagine a number of circumstances in which these generalizations do not apply; e.g., a family might think it a good education in itself for the son to earn his way through school, although they could afford to pay his expenses; or a person might regard it as a sign of personal independence not to have to depend on his parents for his education, despite their ability to pay. Thus, whereas the first generalization stands, the second is subject to a number of interpretations. Even if this is granted, however, it is still true that a person earns part or all of his education whenever it overlapped with his career. Whatever motivation may be ascribed, it is safe to infer from our data whether or not the parents did aid their child's education, even if no conclusion as to their ability to pay is permissible.

[6] This result is corroborated by Walter J. Greenleaf, *op. cit.*, p. 31. According to this study of 40,000 college alumni, a national average of 35 per cent earned nearly all their expenses while attending college, whereas 33 per cent earned one-fourth to one-half. A rough comparison of these data with our own seems feasible if it is remembered that those persons whose career and education overlapped did not necessarily earn all their expenses. In many instances they completed both college and graduate work after entry upon a career, which must mean in many instances that their

This breakdown of educational data lends itself to further analysis.   Since the factor of age and of the changing role of education does not seem to affect the results, it may be useful to analyze the occupational distribution of the fathers in relation to the respondent's educational background.   Among the children of

TABLE XII

Number of respondents listed by father's occupation and extent of college or graduate schooling, before and after entry upon career[a]

Occupation of father	Number of respondents by highest level of education attained			
	Before entry upon career		After entry upon career	
	College*	Graduate work	College*	Graduate work
Laborer (skilled or unskilled)........................	0	0	0	1
Skilled laborer (or mechanic)........................	2	0	1	8
Clerk or salesman.................................	1	0	0	2
Farmer...	11	3	6	25
Small business....................................	10	7	4	12
Large business....................................	7	2	0	4
Government service................................	2	1	0	3
Professional......................................	10	9	4	24
Unknown...	20	20	1	22
Total...	63	42	16	101

[a] In this tabulation all cases are left out in which a person did not go beyond high-school education, whether before or after entry upon his career.   It is felt that this omission is justified here, since the point of interest in this tabulation is the relation between the father's occupation and a person's educational opportunities.   The financing of high-school education does not appear to bear on this point.

* The number of respondents listed under "College" comprises all who have attended college with or without graduation, and in addition all who have attended business or evening schools. Under "Graduate Work" are listed all respondents who did graduate work with or without obtaining higher degrees.   The number of those who did graduate work without acquiring a higher degree is small.

skilled workers, farmers, and, interestingly enough, professionals, economic self-help was of considerable importance in enabling the future administrator to acquire

parents at least helped with their college education, whereas they financed their graduate work themselves.   On the other hand, if Greenleaf's data are regrouped so as to add 16 per cent (estimating roughly those who earned one-half of their expenses rather than one-fourth) to the 35 per cent who earned their way, the resulting 51 per cent is close enough to our own results, although such conjecture can only be suggestive.   It may be added that a similar study, done on a broader basis than was possible here, would provide an opportunity for contributing to our knowledge of social mobility in the United States, at least as far as the role of education is concerned.

an education.   Among the children of small businessmen about as many paid their way as were aided by their families.[7]   Children of large businessmen, on the other hand, tended to complete their education before entering upon their careers.

These compilations indicate a significant difference between the number of cases in which college training and graduate work preceded entry upon a career and the number of cases in which education was acquired after entry upon a career.   Of the 127 administrators who finished their education before beginning their careers,[8] 63, or 49.6 per cent, went to college, whereas 42, or 32.9 per cent, did graduate work.   On the other hand, of the 121 who finished their education after beginning their careers, 3.4 per cent went as far as high school, whereas 16, or 13.2 per cent, went to college, and 101, or 83.4 per cent, did graduate work.   This means, if we again leave the high-school group out of account, that among those finishing their education before beginning their career, 60 per cent went to college, whereas 40 per cent did graduate work.   But among those finishing their education after starting on their careers, just 13.5 per cent went only to college, whereas 86.5 per cent went on to do graduate work.[9]   In the great majority of cases the decision to continue one's education after one's career has been begun is equivalent to an interest in graduate education and the acquisition of higher degrees.   This situation indicates that a considerable number of Federal employees acquire further education while in government service and tends to emphasize the fact that higher administrators are interested in professionalization in the academic sense after having entered upon their careers.[10]   Moreover, of the group as a whole two and one-half times as many acquired their professional training through their own efforts as obtained it through parental help.   This fact speaks in yet another way for the middle and lower middle class origin of the group.

The preceding considerations have been concerned with the social composition and educational background of a sample of higher Federal administrators.   American administrators are typically of rural or small-town origin.   They have come in the majority of cases from families of farmers, small businessmen, and professionals, and over two-thirds of those who obtained a professional education did so by their own efforts.   This characterization of American administrators may now be supplemented by an analysis of the relation between education and government service.

[7] This may very well be more indicative of the stronger development of social ambition in this group than of their greater ability to meet educational expenses.

[8] It should be remembered that this also includes in contrast to Table XII, 22, or 17.5 per cent, who went only to high school.

[9] The difference between these proportions is four times the standard error of the difference.

[10] The general impression about the frequency of post-entry education is, perhaps, somewhat exaggerated.   In our sample 46 out of a possible 248 actually continued their education after entering the Federal service.   The much larger number of persons cited earlier had continued their education after entry upon their careers, but most of them had completed it when they entered the government service; of the 46 who had not, 40 obtained higher degrees during their government service.

EDUCATION AND GOVERNMENT SERVICE

Of what relevance is educational background to careers in the executive branch? Tables XIII, XIV and XV show successively the relationship of the factors of salary level and educational background, age and salary level, and finally salary level and educational background by age-groups. The first of these tabulations

TABLE XIII

Distribution of respondents listed by salary level and education, in 1940

Salary level	No. of respondents by highest level of education attained					
	High school and/or college non-graduate*		College graduate and/or incomplete graduate study		Higher degrees	
	No.	%	No.	%	No.	%
$4,000–$5,550	7	14.8	1	1.8	8	6.1
5,600– 7,950	19	40.4	25	46.2	58	44.2
8,000– Over	21	44.8	28	52.0	65	49.7
Total..................	47	100.0	54	100.0	131	100.0

* This item includes respondents who went to business or evening school but did not obtain a degree.

TABLE XIV

Number of respondents listed by age-group and salary level in 1940

Age-group	Salary level			
	$4,000–5,550	$5,600–7,950	$8,000–Over	Total
30–39	4	15	20	39
40–49	6	50	38	94
50–59	3	25	45	73
60– Over	2	11	15	28
Total...				234

indicates that there is little difference for the group as a whole between those with high-school and college education as against those who have obtained higher degrees, as far as salary levels are concerned. This similarity in salary levels among the three groups of different educational attainments is confirmed for the most part in the other tables. The comparison of salary level and age of respondents shows that the older group is somewhat more frequently represented in the higher salary brackets than the middle-age groups. The difference, however, is small enough to be explained in terms of regular promotions which come with length of service. The only instance in which education rather than age seems to account for a higher salary is found in Table XVIII. A number of respondents in the 30–39 age-group are found in the highest salary bracket, if they have higher

TABLE XV

Number of respondents listed by salary level, highest level of education, and age-group, 1940

Salary level	High school and/or college non-graduate*			College graduate and/or incomplete graduate study*			Higher degrees		
	30–39	40–49	50+	30–39	40–49	50+	30–39	40–49	50+
$4,000–$5,550	1	4	2	0	0	1	2	3	3
$5,600–$7,950	2	11	6	4	11	10	10	28	20
$8,000 and over	0	5	16	1	12	15	20	19	26

* It is convenient to add the corresponding columns under these two headings, if a comparison of respondents with general education as against respondents with professional education is desired. This applies as well to Table XVI.

TABLE XVI

Number of respondents listed by intervals between their last year of schooling and their entry into government service, by length of interval, and year of entry

Entry in government service occurred	Length of intervals in years								Total
	0–5		6–15		16–25		26–over		
	No.	%	No.	%	No.	%	No.	%	
Before 1909	23	74.1	8	25.9	—	—	—	—	31
1910–1919	48	80.0	11	18.3	1	1.7	—	—	60
1920–1929	26	76.4	6	17.7	2	5.9	—	—	34
1930–1939	30	24.8	37	30.6	36	29.8	18	14.9	121
Total									246

degrees.   On the other hand, more respondents of the 50-and-over age-group than of any other age-group are found in the highest salary bracket, even if they have had only a general education.

The growth of executive functions has led to the increasing employment of professionals.   Higher degrees have come to be regarded as a substitute for long experience, although naturally long experience and higher degrees together weigh more heavily in the balance.   However, on the whole professional as against general education accounts surprisingly little for the salary differentials in our sample of administrators. This fact is especially significant in view of the high proportion of professionally trained administrators in the sample.

Although education plays a minor role with regard to advancement in Federal employment, it plays a major role, nevertheless, in the career-patterns of Federal administrators. One of the most important indices of career-patterns is the interval between a person's last year of schooling and the beginning of his career in his chosen employment. The shorter that interval is, the more does education function as preparation for a given type of employment and the more clear-cut

TABLE XVII

Per cent distribution of respondents listed by the extent of their schooling at the time of their entry into government service

Entry into government service	Level of education attained								Total
	High school		College* non-graduate		College graduate		Higher degrees		
	No.	%	No.	%	No.	%	No.	%	
Before 1909	7	22.6	8	25.8	7	22.6	9	29.0	31
1910–1919	11	18.9	16	27.6	23	39.7	8	13.8	58
1920–1929	3	8.9	2	5.9	11	32.3	18	52.9	34
1930–1939	9	6.8	14	11.7	28	23.3	69	57.6	120
Total..									243

* This column includes respondents who attended a business or evening school without obtaining a degree.

one may presume to be a person's intention of making a given type of employment his life career.

The data up to 1919 are too few to be reliable. Moreover, persons who entered government service in their later years during one of the earlier periods have clearly less than an even chance to be included in a sample group of administrators which was selected from the 1940 Official Register. This less-than-even chance makes it remarkable that a little less than 10 per cent of the total sample, representing persons who entered the government before 1919, had had careers of from six to fifteen years duration. The data for the 1920–1929 and 1930–1939 periods indicate that the proportion of persons who entered the government service after a prolonged career in other types of employment has increased considerably since 1930.[11]

11 The *proportion* of those who entered in 1930–39 within a short time after their education was completed, has decreased. The impression prevails that the persons entering government employment since 1930 have been predominantly in the younger age-groups. Although this is not contradicted by the foregoing data, these do suggest that

This consideration of the interval between the end of schooling and entry upon a government career left out of account the extent of schooling among the respondents at the time when they entered the Federal service. As indicated earlier roughly the same proportion of persons in the different age-groups finished their education before as finished it after entry upon a career (Table XI).

With the exception of the 30–39 age-group, professional as against general education did not materially increase the chances of promotion in the civil service. In addition there is the different question about the extent of schooling received at the time when the Federal administrator entered the civil service.

In the period covered the proportion of those who went to high school or to college without completing the latter has sharply declined. The proportion of

TABLE XVIII

Number of respondents listed by the extent of their schooling before entry into government service as related to the number of years between schooling and government service

Length of intervals between schooling and government service	Extent of schooling before govt. service		
	High school and college non-graduate	College graduate	Higher degrees
0–5	34	34	59
6–10	13	7	18
11–15	3	7	13
16–20	3	6	8
21– Over	14	11	13
Total.....................	67	65	111

college graduates has remained relatively more stable. On the other hand, both the number and the proportion of administrators who have higher degrees has increased markedly. Out of the 104 who had higher degrees at the time of their entry into government service, 69 became civil servants between 1930 and 1939. This increasing importance of graduate training in the recruitment of Federal administrators may be brought out by relating the highest level of education attained before government entry to the interval which elapsed between these two career-phases.

The relation between these data and those presented in the preceding table should be noted. Although we have no evidence for the earlier period, we know

persons in the older age-groups have entered government service since 1930 in larger proportions than is commonly believed. It may be added that of the persons (in our sample) entering old-line agencies the number of those who had had a career was approximately the same as of those who entered directly from school. On the other hand, of the persons entering the new government agencies (*i.e.*, those inaugurated during the New Deal) four times as many had had a career before government service as against those who entered on completion of their education.

that in the 1930's a large proportion of older men entered the government. During this same period the number and proportions of respondents with higher degrees had increased considerably as against former periods. The data in Table XVIII underscore these results. Older age at the inception of their government careers is in part because of the greater time devoted to education. And considerably more persons enter the civil service directly from the institutions of learning than in former years.

Education, especially graduate education, has come to play an increasingly important role in the Federal civil service. In relation to advancement education and long experience in government seem to be of equal importance, although graduate training is on the whole more important for the younger than for the older men. It is in keeping with this statement that only nine out of the forty-two who obtained higher degrees after their entry into the Federal service were over forty years of age at the time they received their higher degrees.[12] Moreover, these higher degrees were received throughout the period since 1900. There is, therefore, no undue concentration of higher degrees which were obtained in the period of 1930–1940 after entry into the service. Many of the older men had already acquired their higher degrees either before they entered the Federal service at an earlier time or prior to the expansion of executive functions during the 1930's. Moreover, it appears from our data that the older men were secure enough on the basis of their long experience in the civil service not to fear the competition of the technical experts who became civil servants during the depression. Nevertheless, the increasing importance of higher education as a prerequisite of a civil service career is concomitant with the development of the executive functions of government during the 1930's. This is manifest in the preponderance of persons with higher degrees among those who entered the service during this period.

However, this changing role of education in the civil service cannot by itself account for the apparent increase of older persons among those who began their work in the Federal government since 1930. Although there is no statistical evidence on this point, it seems plausible to assume that the average age at entry was higher after 1930 than before. The implications of this change are analyzed in the following chapter.

---

[12] Seven were between 35 and 39, whereas ten were between 30 and 34, and sixteen were below 30.

CHAPTER V

ALTERNATIVE INCENTIVES IN PRIVATE AND PUBLIC EMPLOYMENT

Since 1930 an increasing proportion of businessmen and of persons with graduate training have entered the Federal service well after the beginning of, and frequently after the midpoint in, their careers. The immediate cause of this development was the depression with its coincident increase of government functions. It is important, therefore, to inquire what effect this development had in terms of the alternative incentives of public as against private employment. It will be useful to discuss this question here as it bears on the developing career-patterns of Federal administrators. (Its wider significance in terms of the prestige of public service will be considered later.)

SALARY DIFFERENTIALS AND EMPLOYMENT SECURITY

It is a popular American *belief* that private employment is preferable to public, in terms of both its greater prestige and its greater financial rewards. However, conclusive *evidence* on this point is difficult to obtain. The most elaborate comparison of compensation for comparable work in private and public employment was made in the late 1920's by the U. S. Personnel Classification Board.[1] The Board reached the conclusion that government salaries in all lower and many of the intermediate brackets compared favorably with compensation for similar work in private employment. On the other hand, the positions of greatest responsibility in business (especially large-scale) were paying from 100 to 500 per cent more than equivalent positions in government. As the Board stated it:

... pay for routine clerical work in the Federal service is somewhat higher than that in private industry. As the elements of judgment and discretion, and finally executive ability, are introduced into the higher classes of employment, the remuneration in the commercial world takes a decided upward trend, and the rate of acceleration is greater than that in the Government salary scheme. In the higher types of employment the salary schedules are so regularly accelerated above Government pay that it is reasonable to conclude that in general greater recognition is given to administrative ability in industry than in the Federal service.[2]

[1] Expert observers have expressed the opinion to the writer that the results of this early survey are still roughly valid. Obviously, wages and salaries in Government and business have changed considerably since that time. But their relationship at different levels has remained stable on |the whole. This has been confirmed by the Commission on Organization of the Executive Branch of the Government (Hoover Commission), *Task Force Report on Federal Personnel* (Washington: Government Printing Office, 1949), pp. 3–6, 30–34. This and the other reports of the Hoover Commission were published after this study was completed.

[2] U. S. Personnel Classification Board, *Closing Report of Wage and Personnel Survey* (Washington: U. S. Government Printing Office, 1931), p. 116. It is interesting to note that a recent study helps to confirm these earlier results in part. In January, 1941, the weekly take-home pay (including overtime) of Federal employees in classified positions

This study has suggested that during the 1930's higher Federal administrators have come in increasing numbers from professional groups, or at any rate from among persons directly after completion of their graduate work. It is of interest

TABLE XIX

Average annual salaries of selected occupations in private and public employment[a]

Occupation	Average salary in	
	Private employment[b]	Public employment[c]
Architecture	$4,200	$3,086
Engineering	4,200	3,169
Journalism	2,250	3,510[d]
Law	3,000	3,993
Medicine	4,600–6,070[e]	4,118
Social work	1,517	2,010
Clerical	1,237–1,574[f]	1,572
Skilled labor[g]	1,430	1,862
Unskilled labor[g]	795	1,195

[a] The data for private and for public employment are all given in median values, unless otherwise noted.

[b] Data for private employment are taken from Harold F. Clark, *Life Earnings in Selected Occupations in the United States* (New York: Harper and Brothers, 1937), pp. 8–9, 107, 110, 131, and are here reprinted by permission of the publisher. Clark's data for the professions are for the period 1920–1929, except where otherwise noted.

[c] The data for public employment are taken from M. L. Smith and K. R. Wright, "Occupations and Salaries in Federal Employment," *Monthly Labor Review* (January 1941), 83–85. All data taken from this study are median annual earnings for 1938.

[d] Journalism does not appear as an occupational category in the study of Federal employment. This category is called instead "Editorial and informational occupations (professional)."

[e] Clark reports these two figures as median values of low and of high medical salaries.

[f] These figures indicate the range of average annual clerical salaries for the period 1928–1934.

[g] The figures for skilled and unskilled labor are mean annual averages based on the period 1920–1936.

to cite the Board's findings about the earnings of these groups, although these data are confined to a comparison of governmental with academic salaries:

The conclusions to be drawn may be summarized as follows: If comparisons are made between the different grades in the Federal service and the different ranks in colleges and universities that have arbitrarily been set as comparable, the Government's professional and scientific workers seem to be receiving higher salaries than are the professional and scientific workers in educa-

was $35.79 as compared with $26.37 of wage-earners in manufacturing, $37.87 in brokerage, $33.29 in street railways and busses, and $32.19 in telephone. See "Salary Trends in Federal Employment," *Monthly Labor Review* (March, 1946), 5. Comparable data on executive positions during the pre-war years are not available, but studies along these lines are in progress in the Civil Service Commission.

tional institutions. If on the other hand, the extracurricular earnings of university professors are added to their salaries and a comparison is then made between the salaries of the two groups, the difference is reversed, for it then appears that the professional and scientific workers in the colleges and universities are receiving a higher compensation than those in the Government service.[3]

These results of the survey of the Personnel Classification Board may be supplemented by reference to the work of Harold P. Clark and the recent study of salary trends in Federal employment referred to above. Clark's work contains salary-data on selected occupations (exclusive of government employment) for the period from 1920–1936. Their bearing on the preceding ·discussion is most

TABLE XIX-A

Average annual salaries of selected occupations in private (1936) and public (1938) employment

Occupation	Average annual salary* in	
	Private employment	Public employment
Architecture...............................	$2,600	$3,086
Engineering................................	2,460	3,169
Journalism.................................	1,875	3,510
Law.......................................	3,013	3,993
Medicine..................................	3,032–3,300	4,118
Business..................................	2,522	
Banking...................................	2,217	
Insurance.................................	2,600	2,248
Merchandising.............................	2,480	
Real Estate...............................	2,017	

* In both columns the average annual salaries are given in median values. The data for public employment are the same as those given in the preceding chart. The data for private employment are taken from W. J. Greenleaf, *Economic Status of College Alumni*, pp. 165–168.

readily appreciated if the average salaries prevailing in the same occupations in private as against public employment are contrasted.

In evaluating these salary-data it should be borne in mind that the period 1920–1929 was on the whole more prosperous economically than 1938. Therefore, the data for private employment should be discounted downwards to some extent to make them comparable with the corresponding government salaries. It is fortunate that the salary-data of another study enable us to make this allowance specific.

It should be noted that Greenleaf's data are derived from a sample-study of 2,144 male college alumni who had graduated in 1928 and were reporting their

[3] *Closing Report of Wage and Personnel Survey*, p. 122. These observations receive further support from the experience of many academicians who obtained higher salaries upon entering government service at the beginning of the war and who sustain substantial cuts if they desire to return to academic work.

salaries for 1936. This fact takes into account the effect of the depression on professional salaries and makes the financial advantage of government employment quite apparent. Since Greenleaf cites average earnings this advantage exists even in the case of businessmen. Many of them apparently earned less on the average during 1936 than the government offered (on the average) to its managerial and administrative personnel ($2,248).[4] Thus, if the downward effect of the depression on salaries in all occupations is taken into account, it is not surprising that professionals as well as businessmen have entered the Federal civil service in increasing proportions during the 1930's.[5] It is said, on the other hand, that public employment has not been attractive to industrialists and large businessmen, among whom it has been customary to look for the executive talent which the government needed.[6] Evidence in the form of testimony by officials and businessmen confirms this, although no systematic study is available on this point.

Salaries are only one aspect of the problem of alternative incentives. Among the other incentives, which are less tangible but hardly less important than salary differentials, are working hours and conditions, vacations and retirement privileges, the opportunities for promotion and tenure. There are, furthermore, specific psychic satisfactions and dissatisfactions which are incident to the "working climate" and the status of the civil servant in America. In the *Wage and Personnel Survey* cited above, government employment was found to compare favorably with private employment in such matters as working hours, vacation and sick-leave privileges, and provisions for retirement. It should be emphasized, however, that these findings may be particularly out of date, since the 1930's have been notable for the advance which private business has made in improving its personnel practices in these respects.

On the problem of security available data are somewhat more ample, although hardly more satisfactory. The problem is important in view of the fact that civil-service employment in other countries has been thought to provide, and in many instances has actually provided, greater security of employment. It is not surprising that this view found widespread acceptance in this country during the depression, although it had hardly been prominent at an earlier time.[7] It is very

---

[4] This comparison of business earnings with those of the managerial and administrative personnel appears plausible in view of the fact that businessmen upon entering government service would presumably be given managerial and administrative responsibilities.

[5] Academic personnel is not listed in the foregoing table, since it was not separately classified in the study of Federal employment. It may be mentioned, however, that Clark's Median Annual Salary for College Teaching (1920–1929) is $2,640, while the Median Annual Salary for all "technical, scientific, and professional" personnel of the government (1938) was $3,137.

[6] This statement is not applicable to the war experience, but it may be doubted whether that experience has changed the situation.

[7] Evidence to show that public employment has come to be regarded in this light, especially under difficult economic circumstances, is provided in the case of Germany by educational statistics. Throughout the 1920's enrollment in the "Rechts- und Staatswissenschaften" (law and political science) outranked enrollment in any of the other fields,

important to distinguish between the belief that public service provides more security than other types of employment and the fact itself. (Both, of course, are "facts" of social significance.) On the latter score the evidence is inconclusive. The findings of the Personnel Classification Board approach the problem through a study of the rate of turnover in public as compared with private employment. The Board argues that the frequency with which separation occurs provides an index of stability. It summarizes its findings as follows:

> In both the clerical, administrative, and fiscal and the professional and scientific services in the District of Columbia the rates of hiring and quitting decline as the grades advance, first precipitately, then slowly, until the higher grades are reached. At that point the rates rise again, rather sharply in the case of the professional and scientific service. Employees in the top grades, in other words, quit and are hired many times more rapidly than is the case with employees quitting or candidates hired in the next lower group of grades. This seems to mean that employees in these services continue quite steadily in employment until they reach the higher grades; and when the relatively responsible positions in these grades are reached, they are soon abandoned for private employment.[8]

In these statements stability and in a sense security are said to be characteristic of public employment in all brackets in which similar positions in private employment pay less. When more pay is offered for the latter, the Federal civil service, particularly in the higher professional and executive positions, becomes unstable. But this meaning of "stability" is not synonymous with "security." If the clerical and administrative employees show a low rate of turnover, then the relatively favorable salaries which government pays at these levels spell "security." However, if the employees in the higher brackets show more turnover, this instability indicates more rather than less security since it means that higher paying jobs continue to be available elsewhere. Thus stability and instability of employment at different levels of the government service may both be an index of security. Data on turnover which are now becoming available do not remedy these difficulties. In many respects they are less satisfactory than the earlier study of the Personnel Classification Board, and some students of Federal employment feel that these earlier results are still substantially valid.[9] No conclusive evidence is,

---

although both medicine and philological and historical departments had been more popular until that time. See Hubert Graven, "Gliederung der Heutigen Studentenschaft nach statistischen Ergebnissen." *Das Akademische Deutschland.* Vol. III (Leipzig: Brockhaus, 1931), p. 347. American evidence on this score is more difficult to evaluate since there is here no clear-cut relation between academic specialization and future occupation. However, the report of the Hoover Commission, *op. cit.*, pp. 7–8, seems to indicate that a preference for Federal employment as a source of security was a phenomenon of the depression. Of 300 former Federal officials, 213 stated that they earned more in their present jobs than they would have earned in the Federal service, and 174 stated that advancement opportunities were greater in private employment. Nevertheless, the experience of many professionals and businessmen with public service during the depression and during the war may well have had more effect on public attitudes than we can discern at present.

[8] *Closing Report of Wage and Personnel Survey*, p. 125.

[9] Data on turnover in Federal employment have been obtained by monthly and annual averages (as compared with industry) and by reasons of separation. The usefulness of these data is restricted further in that they have been ob-

therefore, available on the extent to which the Federal service is in fact a more secure form of employment.[10] Since the evidence on the problem of security in government employment is unsatisfactory, it may be useful to analyze the less tangible incentives of private and public employment.

INTANGIBLE INCENTIVES

During the 1930's (as compared with earlier periods) a proportionately larger number of persons entered the Federal civil service after a prolonged career. Moreover the changing character of executive functions required various kinds of *expertise*. As a result a considerable number of entrants since 1932 came from professional circles.[11] But the fact of outstanding importance is that during this period the average level of compensation from public employment in most types of work exceeded that of private employment.

In the American setting monetary incentives have traditionally been regarded as decisive, and the salary level attained by an individual has been viewed by himself and by his associates as the index of his social status.[12] But in the same setting public employment has been traditionally regarded as second-rate in the sense that the main highway to social and economic advancement was through private enterprise. Higher compensation of public as against private employment during the 1930's created, therefore, many conflicting evaluations.

Naturally this problem did not appear equally formidable to all. To many professionals who entered the civil service, one important attraction has been the opportunity to combine the application of technical skills and specialized knowledge with a concern for nation-wide projects and public welfare. Perhaps this incentive accounts for the many cases in which government service is continued

---

tained only since 1943 and are consequently difficult to use for an understanding of Federal employment in peacetime. For what it may be worth it should be mentioned that during the period from January, 1944 to March, 1946, a comparison of monthly turnover rates between the Federal government and manufacturing industries showed that only in June, 1945 was the accession rate of Federal employment larger than in manufacturing industries. During the same period the separation rates for federal employment exceeded those for private industry only in five out of twenty-seven months. In this over-all sense government employment shows greater stability than private, but this fact allows unfortunately little interpretation. For data on this point cf. the *Federal Employment Statistical Bulletin*, issued monthly by the U. S. Civil Service Commission.

[10] The question whether government service is *believed* to be more secure is not answered thereby. It would appear that to persons for whom the government offers higher-paying jobs than they would otherwise obtain, Federal employment offers both security and advancement-opportunities. Such attitudes appear plausible, at any rate, if the social derivation of our sample group is taken into account. It is important, of course, that the characteristic attitude towards government employment has been that it provides jobs, not that it gives the official dignity and social status. For a view of that sort it is really irrelevant whether government employment is a source of security. Of importance is only the question how far this or any other form of employment is a steady source of jobs. Whether this attitude toward government employment has changed or not, will be considered later.

[11] Detailed data on these two points are presented in the following chapter.

[12] There are, of course, subtler distinctions at the level of community life, as the work of Warner and others has shown. These tend to some extent to mitigate the pervasiveness with which the monetary standard plays a role. But while Warner's emphasis has been on these modifications at the local level, his evidence does not rule out the continued effectiveness of earnings as a status-index in the long run and at the national level.

despite higher financial rewards in private employment. Something of the same motivation seems to have played a role among businessmen. To be sure, they are not experts in the same sense as their professional colleagues, although specialization among businessmen, such as management experts, accountants, and commodity specialists, made major forward strides during this same period. Businessmen were perhaps equally attracted by the sense of fulfillment which comes from participation in national projects concerned with the general welfare. Such inclinations could be enhanced by adverse experiences with the workings of the profit motive, such as the depression provided. But it is misleading to attribute this change in attitudes exclusively to the depression; it seems pertinent to suggest that the depression deepened dissatisfactions which have become associated with the "singleminded pursuit of gain."[13]

"Disinterested service to the public" is only one of the intangible incentives which have come to play a role in the changing character of the American public service. The increasing magnitude of government undertakings helped also to lend the activities of administrators a greater prestige than they had previously attained. And the increasing significance of administrative decision-making (under statutory authority) in turn has attracted a number of men who were more or less unselfishly interested in being close to the powers that be during a period of expanding executive functions.[14]

These important, if intangible, incentives of public employment during the last decade are not in themselves sufficient to account for the "working climate" of the Federal civil service. Positive incentives such as those discussed above may explain the changing attitudes toward public employment and may account in part for the fact that a large proportion of those who entered it since 1932 stayed in the service. As one respondent stated the case:

You stay because you associate with many fine workers, trying hard and honestly to serve the public and do a good job. This confidence in the work you are doing, appreciation of its importance, and pleasure in your associations, keeps you in the government service.

But if these are some of the reasons for the stability in Federal employment, they can be properly understood only if the negative aspects are fully stated. Said the same respondent:

If you ever do administrative work in Government, they never let you leave it. Government administration is a specialized science, abstruse and impenetrable, and becoming more so every day. Only persons of strong will should attempt government administration. You work in an

---

13 For an expression of this attitude see J. A. Krug, "Why I Work for the Government," *This Week* (July 14, 1946)⸱ In the words of one respondent: "Public service offers a great challenge to those whose interest is objectives rather than great financial reward."

14 The significant problem in this respect has less to do with personal motivation than with various aspects of personnel selection in the staffing of key administrative positions.

organization so large you have difficulty in accomplishing changes and improvements of obvious desirability, and under a perpetual glare of Congressional criticism, particularly in election years.

These statements indicate succinctly the ambivalence of positive and negative incentives which characterize the higher Federal service. Professionals and businessmen who have come to work in Washington are unanimous in their complaints. Government work is slow, full of red tape, "improvements of obvious desirability" are sometimes impossible and always difficult of accomplishment, each administrative action requires elaborate safeguards and "coordination" or "clearance," improvisation is shunned, initiative atrophied, and so on. Moreover, wartime experience has shown that there are some essential differences between government and business administration. Businessmen who have entered the government found it difficult to adjust themselves to the frequent reorganizations characteristic of government. They were accustomed to long-established business organizations in which reorganizations are, if not necessarily less frequent, at any rate less sweeping. To work in the "glare of Congressional and public criticism" has stood in marked contrast to the relative seclusion from public notice of most business transactions.[15]

To a person with academic background and to the professional specialist the negative incentives of civil-service work appear, perhaps, different. That work attracts the specialist because of the opportunity to work on a large scale and because of a sense of participation that academic work does not yield. Yet the size of the administrative agencies and departments makes it more difficult for him to feel that his work is worth while. Moreover, he often finds it difficult to divorce himself from administrative considerations, and administrators voice the constant complaint that technicians show a decided inability to operate effectively in the "administrative climate." As a result, a problem of considerable magnitude lies in the search for technicians with administrative ability who are sufficiently expert to understand the work of a scientific bureau and sufficiently "administrative" to make it function smoothly. It need only be mentioned that this problem is aggravated whenever the technical capacity itself involves the policy implications of the administrative process, as in the case of the lawyers.[16]

---

[15] For a discussion of wartime experience with businessmen as administrators cf. Herbert Emmerich, "The Search for Executive Talent," in L. D. White, ed., *Civil Service in Wartime* (Chicago: University of Chicago Press, 1945), pp. 36–41.

[16] Cf. Fritz Morstein-Marx, "The Lawyer's Role in Public Administration," *Yale Law Journal*, LV (April, 1946), 500 (reprinted here by permission of the Editor): ". . . administrative law must seek its aim in furnishing guidance and imposing restraint in the exercise of authority wherever the administrative process affects the individual. The agency lawyer is not merely the servant of regulation. He is tied also into the execution of a large variety of service functions administered for the benefit of one or another clientele. . . ." But "the lawyer is a good administrator by coincidence only; he is not specially trained for administration, and, indeed, the narrow and specialized legal education he has received may be considered to be particularly unsuited for the types of problems to be faced." The latter quotation is taken from Vincent M. Barnett, "Modern Constitutional Development: A Challenge to Administration," *Public Administration Review*, IV (1944), 163. (Reprinted here by permission of the Editor.)

BUSINESS CONDUCT AND THE ADMINISTRATIVE PROCESS

The evidence which has been reviewed so far does not indicate that higher Federal administrators in America constitute a cohesive social group. Their family background and educational experience are too diverse to be the basis of a common outlook and concerted action. Moreover, a review of the incentives which have prompted them to enter and to stay in the civil service does not suggest that invidious motivations have played in their case a conspicuous role. Such evidence does not, however, answer the larger question of the relationship between bureaucracy and the exercise of power. A further step toward an analysis of this relationship lies in an examination of the significant differences in the administrative process of government and business. Comparative analyses addressing this topic have in the past been associated with two major themes: a contrasting of the role of bureaucracy in business and government, and a technical and/or psychological exploration of "administrative pathology" in either type of organization.

Previous attempts at comparing bureaucracy in business and government have been marred not only by partisanship, but by a failure to identify the historical periods for which the organizations of business and government were being compared. This has led to the predicament that some students find the evil of bureaucracy only in business or only in government.[17] It is hardly a solution of the problem to suggest that bureaucracy is to be found in both. While certain administrative difficulties are characteristic of all organizations, the differences are perhaps more noteworthy than the likenesses. They are attested by the businessmen who have entered the Federal civil service and are confirmed by many administrators who comment on the difficulties which businessmen have encountered in Washington.[18] Such evidence is difficult to dismiss on the ground that the principles of management and organization in business and government are similar.[19] It is reinforced by frequent statements to the effect that businessmen who enter the higher Federal service are too ready to make quick decisions, whereas experienced administrators know that their actions must be "cleared" before being put into effect. It is illustrated by the obvious contrast between the purchasing agent of a large concern and the purchasing agent of the Federal government.

---

[17] Cf. my "Bureaucracy and the Problem of Power," *Public Administration Review*, V (Summer, 1945), 200, note 1.

[18] For discussion of the contrast between business and government, cf., O. H. von der Gablentz, "Industriebuerokratie," *Schmoller's Jahrbuch*, L (1926), 539–572; Edgar Landauer, "Kapitalistischer Geist und Verwaltungsbuerokratie in Oeffentlichen Unternehmungen," *Schmoller's Jahrbuch*, LIV (1930), 505–521; Kurt Wiedenfeld, *Kapitalismus und Beamtentum* (Berlin: Walter de Gruyter, 1932); E. G. Cahen-Salvador, "La situation materielle et morale des fonctionnaire," *Revue politique et parlementaire*, CXXXIX (1926), 315–338; Marshall E. Dimock and Howard K. Hyde, *Bureaucracy and Trusteeship in Large Corporations* (Monograph 11 of the Temporary National Economic Committee; Washington: Government Printing Office, 1940); Werner Sombart, *Beamtenschaft und Wirtschaft* (Berlin: Verlagsanstalt des Deutschen Beamtenbundes, 1927).

[19] This contention is made by Marshall E. Dimock, *The Executive in Action* (New York: Harper and Brothers, 1945), pp. 5–8.

The former has at his disposal regular accounts for gratuities, without which ordinary business transactions cannot be effected, while the latter is exceedingly scrupulous in his business transactions for the government so that they do not appear questionable on any ground whatsoever.

It is important to note the principle which underlies these differences. Profit and loss of the business enterprise depend more or less directly on the price fluctuations of the world market. Its success is indicated by its profits; there is no guarantee against losses. The actions of the businessman are oriented towards these criteria of business conduct, and he can, if expedient, treat each transaction as a case by itself, deciding to buy or sell on a moment's notice as market conditions dictate it. The administrator, on the other hand, strives to realize through the activities of his agency some conception of general welfare. His success can obviously not be measured in terms of profit, but will be judged by himself and the public in terms of the social and political context in which it has its place. It is not denied that success, efficiency, and accomplishment of real service to the public are a possibility inherent in the administrative process; but their indices and their rewards differ from those of the business enterprise.[20] The two types of organizations tend to emphasize certain traits. For the businessman quick decision-making often spells the difference between success and failure. For the administrator it is essential that all the possibilities be carefully weighed before a course of action is decided upon. A wrong decision about business transactions does not constitute a precedent; the losses resulting from it may be recouped. A wrong administrative decision does constitute a precedent; and although it is possible to reverse it at a later date, such changes in administrative action are regarded by the public as arbitrary. Paradoxically enough the checking and re-checking of administrative decisions which safeguards against policy-reverses at the price of delayed action is regarded as red tape.[21]

[20] von Mises' book *Bureaucracy* (New Haven: Yale University Press, 1944) contains little more than an elaboration of this point. He is apparently quite unaware of the techniques of administrative supervision and the various public opinion polls used to ascertain the success of administrative programs. What is more, he commits the unpardonable logical error of contrasting the *real* workings of the administrative process (as he understands them) with the *ideal* operation of the competitive enterprise. Cf. in this connection C. H. Pritchett's statement about the differences in accounting practice between business and government in his article, "The Government Corporation Control Act of 1945," *American Political Science Review*, XL (June, 1946), 502–505. See also Hoover Commission, *Federal Business Enterprises* (Washington: Government Printing Office, 1949), pp. 106–112, where the basic conflict between private accounting practices and public policy is forcefully stated.

[21] Cf. the testimony of Chester Bowles before the Joint Committee on the Organization of Congress: "I have been interested in the difference between Government administrative problems and business administrative problems. I do not think there is much we can do about the handicap under which Government works, but in business you work quietly in an organization of top people. You decide that some risk is worth taking, you see gains to be made by that risk if it succeeds. You evaluate the risks and move ahead aggressively and vigorously to get that done. Then if you see it is not working very well you modify it, and if you again see it is not working very well you abandon it. When you get through, though, no one knows about it but the people in the organization, and year after year the corporation has a yardstick with which to measure its profit statement; and assuming it carries out its social problems with the employees, you have a yardstick with which to measure the successes and the mistakes.

"In Government administration, you make your decisions in public. Therefore, first of all, you are hesitant to

Such differences between the operation of business and government do not deserve to be overemphasized at the present time. These differences have decreased with the development of large-scale business.[22] In his analysis of the contrast Wiedenfeld has pointed out that the administrator is distinguished from the businessman primarily in the sense that the former is consumer-minded, both for himself and for his public, while the latter is ideally production-minded in both respects. It is characteristic of the consumer that he is interested primarily in stability of prices, wages, and working conditions. It follows, therefore, that the attempts of businessmen to secure their enterprises from the effects of market fluctuations through monopolistic practices inevitably re-enforces bureaucratic tendencies in their organizations. Businessmen become in this sense consumer-minded when they favor the security of steady profits in preference to the uncertainty of spectacular profits and spectacular losses. To be sure, this does not mean that business executives become consumer-minded in all respects. Wiedenfeld, however, writes:

It is a socially significant corollary of business concentration . . . that the prospects are diminished for its managerial personnel to advance into independent executive positions. Consequently, even here the feeling of initiative, which lies at the basis of all willingness to take risks, will be superseded by union sentiments. This change in attitude and ambition cannot fail to affect the productive effort of this managerial personnel. Reluctance to take responsibility and the emphasis on the correct execution of orders coming from above are the inevitable result. . . . And this in turn will have the consequence that the leading executive positions of the largest

---

move. You say the penalty for being wrong is pretty serious. The Associated Press, United Press, Fulton Lewis, Jr., everybody, is watching to see what you do. And so first you hesitate and then you move ahead. Then, suppose it does not work out very well. You do one of two things: You pretend it is working better than it is, or you get frantic and say, 'If I wait, it may work better. . . .'

"You feel, if you postpone the issue, some of it may be solved. Therefore, you hang on to your mistakes sometimes too long in Government administration, which is a goldfish bowl, and there is nothing you can do about that. You have to try to get people in the Government with enough courage to move ahead, because one way not to make mistakes is not to do anything. You have got to move, and when you move, as an administrator, you are always taking some risks, but there is nothing you can do about that." See U. S. Congress, Joint Committee on the Organization of Congress. *Hearings Pursuant to H. Con. Res. 18.*, 79th Congress, 1st sess., (Washington: Government Printing Office, 1945), pp. 738-739. A similar analysis is presented by Kurt Wiedenfeld, *op. cit.*, pp. 10-19. It is of interest, however, that Wiedenfeld carries his comparative analysis a step further into the problem of financial compensation, where the differences between business and government become historical and national rather than systematic. He shows that civil servants are paid in proportion to their "costs of production," *i.e.*, to the costs of their education, and in terms of what is regarded as appropriate to their status in society. Wiedenfeld recognizes that the latter consideration is more prominent in Germany than in England, and we might add more prominent in England than in the United States. German literature on the civil service is replete with considerations of the relation between government salaries and the standard of living which is appropriate for a public official. American literature tends to emphasize that government must raise its salaries if it is to succeed in attracting the highest executive talent.

[22] Even for the earlier period some doubts have been expressed whether the picture of the "heroic *entrepreneur*," who is always used as the opposite of the "cautious administrator," is an accurate portrayal of the businessmen of early and high capitalism. See Fritz Redlich, *History of American Business Leaders* (Ann Arbor: Edwards Brothers, 1940), I, ch. i, who expresses some doubts whether the German and the American business leaders of the same period were really men of the same type. For a statement of the theory cf. Joseph Schumpeter, *Communism, Socialism and Democracy* (New York: Harper and Brothers, 1942), pp. 121-143. The striking differences between highly capitalistic countries in their approach to business conduct are analyzed in Hermann Levy, *Volkscharakter und Wirtschaft* (Leipzig: B. G. Teubner, 1926).

enterprises will not be filled by their own managerial personnel, but rather by outsiders, who in heading up small enterprises were able to preserve their desire for independent action and who could there prove their ability. And that will deteriorate still further the promotional prospects of the managerial personnel in large enterprises, who will clamor all the more for security and a bureaucratic insurance of their positions.[23]

Other tendencies among businessmen point the same way. All efforts to transform through monopolistic practices a profit-and-loss system into a profit system, all attempts to become independent of the market or to control it, the whole idea of reasonable profits which should be secured are so many reinforcing tendencies of business bureaucracy. Practices about the salaries of top executives tell the same story. They tend to secure part of their wealth against the risks of their own enterprises by real estate transactions and transfer of property titles to their wives. They prefer to be paid very high salaries in compensation for their work, rather than run the risk of taking a share of the profits.[24] Thus security of profits through monopolistic practices encourages in business the duplication of functions, the clearing of decisions, the reluctance to take responsibility which we associate with bureaucracy in its invidious sense. And these tendencies are bound to affect the conduct of the executive personnel, not only within the business but in their personal financial dealings. Consequently, the contrasts between business conduct and the bureaucratic aspect of the administrative process diminish in proportion as industrial concentration grows. On the other hand, the multiplication of functions in the executive branch leads to the penetration of business practices into many phases of administration.[25]

Although the differences between business and government have diminished, it is essential to recognize that one difference remains. Democratic administration may exceed its delegated powers, because it can discriminate against individuals and groups through inaction and because the supervisory controls of the government are insufficient. In either case it is subject to publicity and public criticism. A business enterprise may exercise its power within such limits as the passive resistance of the public, the wide-meshed network of legal restraints, and its own anticipations of adverse consequences will prescribe. (The last item covers such factors as competition, possible publicity, and the like.) These differences depend upon the nature of the checks which control busines conduct and ad-

---

[23] Wiedenfeld, *op. cit.*, pp. 29–30. (My translation).

[24] This attitude may change, to be sure, when income taxes become steep enough to make these risks worth while.

[25] Cf. the comprehensive appraisal of government corporation by Leonard D. White, *Introduction to the Study of Public Administration* (New York: The Macmillan Co., 1939), pp. 124–141. See also the interesting account of the mixture of administrative and commercial considerations in German government corporation by Edgar Landauer, *op. cit.* This interpretation of business and administration is new only in its present form. It was a characteristic of government administration in the past whenever this was closely related to the King's household or to the actual operation of the national economy. Sombart reports that in Austria civil servants used to work as travelling salesmen in search for buyers of Austrian commodities, down to the presentation of samples and sales talk. See Sombart, *op. cit.*, p. 5.

ministrative action respectively. Neither type of organization is all-powerful. But the checks on large-scale business enterprises are more intangible, and presumably less effective, than the checks on the administrative exercise of governmental power.[26]

[26] No comprehensive comparison of controls has yet been attempted. For an analysis of the business side see Robert A. Brady, *Business as a System of Power*, (New York: Columbia University Press, 1943), pp. 298–310, 317–319, *et passim*.

CHAPTER VI

CAREER-LINES OF HIGHER FEDERAL ADMINISTRATORS

The preceding chapter has been concerned with the changing pattern of incentives in private and public employment. We may now analyze the interest-orientation and occupational experience of our sample group, which illustrates the alternative incentives discussed earlier.

OCCUPATIONAL DISTRIBUTION PRIOR TO GOVERNMENT SERVICE

The occupational experience of the group is indicated by the occupational distribution of respondents before their entry into the Federal service, special reference being made to the periods during which their entry occurred. In Table XX, the column for the 1890–1909 period should be discounted since too many administrators of this older age-group have retired or died. But the differences in the occupational distribution of respondents entering the government service during the other periods are striking. The percentage of persons who were gainfully occupied before entering the Federal service in 1930–40 exceeds in each occupation the corresponding percentage of persons entering during the preceding period. This fact is especially noticeable in the groups comprised of businessmen, government workers other than Federal, lawyers, engineers, university teachers, newspaper men, and representatives of trade associations.

It may be useful to present a summary of this table which highlights the main contrasts. The data in Table XXI confirm the growing importance of professionals in the Federal civil service and specify the occupational categories from which proportionally more administrators have come during the 1930's. This trend indicates a change in the career-patterns of higher Federal administrators. It is commonly thought that the proportion of persons going into government service directly after their education has been completed has increased during 1930–40. The present study does not provide conclusive evidence on this point.[1] It does show, however, that the proportion of persons who entered the Federal service after a prolonged career has increased. Even if the proportion of young persons entering Federal employment directly from school remained the same since 1920, the simultaneously larger proportion of older entrants still differentiates the career-patterns characteristic of administrators who entered the Federal service since 1930. Therefore, these career-patterns of the respondents as well as the time of their entry into government service are of interest. Table XXII shows the distribution of respondents by selected occupation prior to their government service

---

[1] Cf. Chapter IV, note 11.

TABLE XX

Number and per cent of respondents listed by occupations prior to government service and by period during which entry occurred[a]

Principal occupation prior to government service	Periods during which respondents entered government service					
	1890–1909		1910–1929		1930–1940	
	No.	%	No.	%	No.	%
Laborer (unskilled and semi-skilled).............	—	—	1	1.1	—	—
Skilled laborer (mechanic).....................	—	—	—	—	—	—
Clerk or salesman.............................	3	—	7	7.8	1	.8
Farmer......................................	1	—	—	—	3	2.3
Small businessman............................	—	—	4	4.4	10	7.9
Large businessman............................	—	—	4	4.4	8	6.2
Government service						
a Federal (other than in executive branch).....	—	—	1	1.1	2	1.6
b. State....................................	—	—	6	6.7	7	5.4
c. Local....................................	—	—	—	—	7	5.4
Professional						
a. College teaching.........................	1	—	8	8.9	16	12.6
b. Engineering.............................	—	—	3	3.3	10	7.9
c. Law.....................................	2	—	5	5.6	26	20.3
d. Teaching (other than college)..............	1	—	5	5.6	3	2.3
e. Administrative research and surveys.........	—	—	—	—	3	2.3
f. Banking.................................	—	—	—	—	4	3.1
g. Journalism...............................	—	—	1	1.1	11	8.6
h. Representative of trade assn.[b].............	—	—	1	1.1	8	6.2
i. All others...............................	—	—	6	6.7	4	3.1
Education[c]						
a. High school.............................	7	—	11	12.2	—	—
b. College.................................	7	—	21	23.3	1	.8
c. Graduate work...........................	4	—	6	6.7	4	3.1
Total......................................	26		90		128	

[a] This tabulation is concerned with the principal careers of the respondents prior to their entry into government service; that is to say, either the occupation in which they had been engaged for the longest number of years, or in which they had been engaged prior to their entry in the Federal service, whichever of the two was higher in the occupational hierarchy. The term "higher" here as elsewhere refers to such cases as, for example, the career of a respondent who had been a clerk for seven years and a bank vice-president for five years before entering the government. In this instance his last job was counted. In all doubtful cases the first of the two principles of tabulation was adhered to.

[b] This item does not include representatives of other types of private associations.

[c] Under "Education" are listed all respondents who entered government service directly after their schooling (at whatever level). In this table "College" includes all respondents who went to business or evening school as well as the "College Non-Graduates." Under "Graduate Work" are included all respondents who did graduate work, whether or not they obtained higher degrees.

in terms of whether they entered it shortly after their schooling or after a prolonged career.

TABLE XXI

Number and per cent of respondents listed by selected principal occupations and by period during which entry into Federal service occurred

Principal occupation	Period of entry			
	1910–1929		1930–1940	
	No.	%	No.	%
Business	8	8.8	18	14.1
Government Service (other than executive branch)	7	7.8	16	12.4
Professionals	28	31.2	77	66.2
Representatives of trade associations	1	1.1	8	6.2
Student (entering government directly from educational institutions)	38	42.2	5	3.9

TABLE XXII

Number and per cent of respondents listed by selected occupations and by career-patterns

Principal occupation	Respondents entering government service*			
	From school and/or after initial Employment		After prolonged Career[a]	
	No.	%	No.	%
Business	3	4.0	23	16.2
Government Service (other than executive branch)	3	4.0	20	14.1
Professional	21	27.5	84	59.3
Representative of Trade Assn	—	—	9	6.3
Student (entering govt. directly from educational institutions)	43	56.6	—	—

* Temporary employment during schooling is left out of account in all tabulations. But in setting up the types of careers it was found necessary to allow for a certain amount of initial employment. Thus, if a college graduate becomes a salesman for two years after graduation and then enters the government where he has stayed ever since, he was counted in the first column. Employment was regarded as "initial" in this sense, whenever it was either less than five years in duration and/or when it occurred before the 25th year, whichever was decisive.

[a] The category "After Prolonged Career" includes not only persons who entered government after a career but also those whose service was discontinuous, alternating between private and public employment.

It should be remembered that out of the 142 who entered government service after a prolonged career, 39 did so before 1932, whereas 103 joined the Federal service from 1932 on. The changing career-pattern is related to the turning-point of 1932, but it had been in the making before that time. The quick expansion of government employment and the pressure of economic circumstances were important factors. But the major changes in the public service which have occurred since 1932 are not only the result of the depression. The growth of functions in the executive with its attendant problems of large-scale administration had long been in the making. The data on occupational background before entry

TABLE XXIII

*Number of respondents listed by types of degrees received**

Degree received	Number of respondents receiving	
	College graduation degrees	Higher degrees
B.A.	85	—
LL.B.	—	69
B.S.	46	—
M.A.	—	34
Ph.D.	—	25
M.S.	—	12
LL.M.	—	11
S.J.D.	—	6
C.E.	—	4
D.C.L.	—	3
M.P.L.	—	3
Ph.B.	3	—
LL.D.	—	3
M.B.A.	—	2
M.D.	—	2
B.D.	—	2
Total	134	176

* This tabulation excludes the 28 honorary degrees received by the respondents, among which are 10 honorary LL.D. and 14 honorary D.Sc. degrees.

into the Federal service are important in that they give a picture of the interests and affiliations of the group. Occupational choice is, however, only a very broad index of interest-orientation and personal association. Educational specialization and membership in voluntary associations provide additional clues in this respect. It is, therefore, important to indicate first the diversity of educational specialization in this group of administrators.

This diversity may be shown by tabulating the number and kind of degrees which the group has obtained. As was noted earlier, 52 out of 242 administrators are college graduates, whereas 134 acquired higher degrees. These 186 received the degrees listed in Table XXIII.

It appears that out of 176 higher degrees which were received by 134 Federal administrators about one-half are law degrees.[2]   However, only 22 out of the 242 respondents were employed as lawyers, although 50 additional respondents are among the recipients of law degrees.   This proportion of lawyers (29 per cent) in

TABLE XXIV

Number of club memberships listed by types of clubs among 248 respondents

Types of clubs	Number of club memberships	
I. Social clubs		
a. Sports clubs...	20	
b. Lodges...	34	
c. University clubs and fraternities.............................	81	
d. Recreational clubs...	77	212
II. Business associations...		28
III. Professional associations		
a. Bar associations...	49	
b. "Public Administration Associations"........................	86	
c. Political science associations...............................	17	
d. Associations of natural scientists (including engineers)...........	65	
e. Social work assn...	21	
f. Medical assn..	10	
g. Economic, statistical and accounting assn......................	47	
h. Sociological and historical societies..........................	9	
i. Journalistic assn..	14	
j. Conservation societies......................................	19	
k. Professional academic associations...........................	14	
l. Miscellaneous assn...	8	359
IV. Others		9
Total..		608

a sample of Federal administrators (regardless of whether they *worked* as lawyers in 1940 or not) is comparable to the proportion of lawyers among our state legislators,[3] but was far below their proportion in the Congress.[4]

Another index of interest-orientation and occupational affiliation is contained in a compilation of club memberships of Federal administrators.   This indicates their predominantly professional interests.   The figures in Table XXIV are for the

[2] In accordance with common practice all law degrees have been classified as higher degrees in the preceding tabulations.

[3] This percentage varied between 21 per cent and 35 per cent among the different states. See W. T. R. Fox, "Legislative Personnel in Pennsylvania," *The Annals*, CXCV (January, 1938), 36, where comparative figures for the various states are given.   According to E. P. Herring there were 26.7 per cent lawyers among his sample of 142 Federal Commissioners.   See his *Federal Commissioners* (Cambridge: Harvard University Press, 1936), p. 109.

[4] Of the Senators and Representatives of the 77th Congress, 311 out of 665, or 46.7 per cent, listed their former occupation as "lawyer." See M. M. McKinney, "The Personnel of the 77th Congress," *American Political Science Review*, XXXVI (1942), Table VI.

group as a whole.   The breakdown that is of greatest interest, perhaps, indicates that roughly the same number of respondents (about 143) belong to the social clubs and the professional associations (they are, of course, in many instances not the same persons).   Administrators who are members of professional associations frequently belong to two or three such associations.   Many of them comment that they could not afford to keep up their membership in social clubs.   When they had to choose, they preferred the professional associations.[5]

The data indicate at the same time the predominance and the diversity of professional interests among higher Federal administrators.   In view of the well-known differences in occupational interest and intellectual orientation among lawyers, administrators, natural scientists, newspapermen, and others, it seems reasonable to advance the hypothesis that the increased employment of professionals in the Federal service has not resulted in its professionalization.   Further considerations bearing on this point will be advanced in Chapters VIII and IX.

PROMOTIONAL OPPORTUNITIES

The problem of incentives has been examined so far in terms of the financial attractiveness of the civil service and in terms of its intangible rewards.   The data in the preceding section indicate also to which occupational groups these incentives of government service have proved effective during recent years.   But if an increasing number of persons with prolonged careers in private employment are hired by the government, they immediately come into top positions.   Apparently this situation prevents employees in the lower brackets from moving up.   Consequently the problem of retaining government employees in the service as well as that of attracting them to it has beset government personnel officers.

How much of the practice of hiring employees at top levels is an indispensable concomitant of the rapid multiplication of executive functions?   It may facilitate the rapidity with which new agencies can be set up and made to operate quickly. Yet it is an open question whether the same results could be obtained by recruiting top administrators from within the service.   It is commonly thought that this hiring policy was widespread in the pre-war civil service, but evidence on this point does not clearly support this belief.   The problem is one not only of recruitment but of internal personnel adjustment.   The opportunity to join the government service in high-bracket positions was an obvious incentive to professionals after prolonged careers.   The same fact would only rarely function as a deterrent to college graduates who begin in P-1 positions.[6]   That opportunity

[5] In view of the middle-aged character of the group, the small number of lodge memberships is of interest.

[6] This assertion is not contradicted, I believe, by an older study which indicated that many students were reluctant to enter government service because of a "lack of promotional prospects."   There is no reason to believe that students are fully informed about promotional opportunities.   They are likely to react rather to the "Horatio Alger" version of business success and to confuse the top salaries in business and government with the promotional prospects in both

would, however, act as a deterrent to younger persons, once they had entered the government service and found the possibilities of promotion limited. A realization of restricted opportunities may come at a time when a person is no longer able to change his position. This fact applies especially to persons who have had few opportunities before entering the government service to establish contacts which are useful in obtaining private employment. However, it is impossible to estimate from the data at hand to what extent this is a major dilemma or a matter of individual instances.

The difficulties involved in finding an answer to this problem are demonstrated by a study of 1,920 Washington P-1 employees, who entered the government service from 1935–1939. The study revealed that 744, or 39 per cent, received promotions during this period. These promotions are analyzed in considerable detail; however, no conclusion was feasible as to how favorably or unfavorably this proportion compared with other types of employment. The 744 employees who were promoted compared with 289, or 15 per cent, whose service with the government was terminated during the same period.[7] It might be thought that the promotional opportunities of the lower grades are diminished if a larger number of persons are appointed at the higher rather than at the lower professional grades. But no conclusive evidence has been forthcoming to show that promotions are more infrequent and separations more numerous among P-1 employees than they would have been if fewer professional employees had been appointed at the higher grade. There is also no evidence to indicate that the hiring of outside professional personnel was in general preferred to the promotion of civil servants. It may well be, on the other hand, that a number of circumstances such as authorization difficulties and lack of flexibility in intra-governmental personnel policies may have had the same effect.

Although it is doubtful whether the expectation of promotion plays a considerable role as an incentive in recruitment, the promotion-policy itself may foster the stability of public employment. The record of government service of higher Federal administrators provides a clue to the adequacy of promotion, at least for the higher Federal service. Their high positions are indicative of the availability of alternative employment possibilities, both because of their abilities and because of the multiplicity of their contacts. Their long record of government service suggests that, among other factors, the chances of promotion within the govern-

---

types of employment. The study referred to is briefly reviewed in William E. Mosher and J. Donald Kingsley, *Public Personnel Administration* (New York: Harper and Brothers, 1936), p. 42. The whole problem is discussed by W. F. Littlejohn, "Promotion and Transfer Opportunities and Methods in the Federal Administration," in U. S. Committee on Civil Service Improvement, *Documents and Reports to Accompany Report on Civil Service Improvement* (Washington: Government Printing Office, 1942), III, Part 2, 26–27.

[7] For further details see W. F. Littlejohn, "Promotional History of P-1 Appointees," *op. cit.*, especially the tables on pp. 12 and 24. Cf. alone the discussion of promotional opportunities in business, Ch. V, p. 42.

ment have been satisfactory for them.[8] In view of these considerations it is of interest to examine the service record of this sample group.

This service record is not by itself sufficient as an index of stability in government employment. A group of higher Federal administrators, however chosen, would always contain only a small number of persons who recently entered the Federal service. A better index of stability is the extent to which service has been continuous in one executive department or another. Such continuity indicates that the possibilities of advancement from within have been satisfactory. Frequent transfers, on the other hand, are not evidence of a lack of promotional opportunities since transfers to other departments are frequently synonymous with promotions.

TABLE XXV

Number of respondents listed by years of government service

Years of service	Number of respondents
1	10
2	7
3– 4	12
5– 6	40
7– 8	53
9–10	6
11–15	14
16–20	24
21–25	32
26 and over	49
	247

The data contained in Table XXVI indicate that the stability in Federal employment has not noticeably decreased since 1932. The tabulation of the respondents' service records (Table XXV), shows two declining frequency distributions which are clearly divided by the year 1932. In other words, there is a clustering of respondents who have been in the Federal civil service since before 1914; the number of respondents who have entered the service since that time steadily declined until 1932. Another large group of respondents entered Federal employment in that year, and again the number of respondents who joined the government since 1933 declined from then on.

This break in the frequency distribution of the group's service record is not in-

---

[8] It should be noted that this argument does not by the same token apply to persons who entered government service since 1933 directly after their schooling. Moreover, this is a statistical index of adequate promotional opportunities. Such an index does not preclude the possibility that these opportunities may have been felt to be unsatisfactory although they were sufficient.

dicative of a change in the stability of the Federal service.   If a horizontal line is drawn in Table XXVI after the eighth year (1932), it will be seen that the total number of respondents who have had no transfer or one transfer, and so on, is not significantly different above from below the line.   Thus 78 of those who joined the civil service since 1932 stayed in one department as against 62 who had entered government service before that year (35 of the former and 38 of the latter group made one transfer since entering the government service).   Of the whole group, 56.7 per cent stayed in one department, whereas 29.6 per cent made one transfer.[9]

TABLE XXVI

Number of respondents listed by years of government service and number of interagency transfers

Years of service	Number of transfers*						
	0	1	2	3	4	5	6
1	10						
2	6	1					
3– 4	11	1					
5– 6	24	15	1				
7– 8	27	18	7	1			
9–10	3	1	1	1			
11–15	9	5	–	–			
16–20	9	9	3	2	1		
21–25	18	7	4	2	–		
26–Over	23	16	7	1	–	–	2
Total..........	140	73	23	8	1		2

* The respondents listed under "0" transfers stayed in the same department throughout their government service.   One transfer means that they have served in two departments since entering the government service, and so on.   Cases in which a respondent has served in two departments although he remained in the same bureau, for example, Weather Bureau, were tabulated as one transfer.

OCCUPATIONAL OPPORTUNITIES AND CHOICES DURING AND AFTER
GOVERNMENT SERVICE

The relative stability in the employment record of the group permits the inference that the incentives within the higher Federal service have been relatively

[9] The latter percentage should be discounted to some extent since it includes a number of cases where the respondent stayed in his bureau while the bureau itself, due to reorganization, was transferred to another department. If this allowance is made, it appears that the proportion of transfers between different government departments and agencies for the group as a whole is strikingly similar to the transfer-pattern between the divisions within the bureau to which reference was made earlier (Chap. IV, p. 32).   For this bureau a separate tabulation was made of the transfer-record of the division chiefs, assistant division chiefs, section chiefs, program directors, etc., and this evidence would tend to support the view that the transfer record of administrative managers within agencies is similar to that between government agencies.

TABLE XXVII
Number and per cent of outside employment-offers listed by types of employment[a]

Types of employment	Number and per cent of job-offers received	
	Number	Per cent
Manufacturing...	39	15.7
Business (other than manufacturing)		
a. Food industry... 7		
b. Airlines.. 5		
c. Insurance... 6		
d. Wholesale trade...................................... 3		
e. Transportation....................................... 3		
f. Public utilities...................................... 4		
g. Export... 2		
h. Cooperatives.. 2		
i. Department store..................................... 3		
j. Movies... 1		
k. Chemical firm.. 1		
l. Corporate farming.................................... 1		
m. Unspecified... 7	45	18.2
Banking..	16	6.4
Universities (teaching, administration, research)................	35	14.1
Publicity work		
a. Publishing (newspaper, magazine, books)................. 16		
b. Radio... 9		
c. Advertising agency.................................... 5		
d. Promotion.. 1		
e. Representative of private assn.[b]....................... 8	39	15.8
Legal firms..	23	9.3
Other government service[c]................................	16	6.4
Professional work		
a. Engineering... 6		
b. Social service....................................... 5		
c. Marketing research................................... 5		
d. Personnel management................................ 4		
e. Management consultant................................ 4		
f. Others... 4	28	11.2
Miscellaneous..	7	2.9
Total..	248	100.0

[a] These data have been derived from the answers to the question: "Have you ever been offered a job in private employment since you have joined the government service? Indicate the type of business from which such offers have come." One hundred eighty-four respondents answered this question; of these, 32 indicated that they had not received such offers. Thus the 248 job-offers listed above were received by 152 respondents, which is impressive even if the number of offers is discounted somewhat, since some of these may not have been "serious."

[b] This item includes three offers from trade associations, two from the CIO-PAC, two from private foundations, one from the Veterans of Foreign Wars.

[c] Offers for "other government service" were unspecified in five cases; four came from foreign governments, two from UNRRA, one from AMG, one from the UN; three were for "city planning" positions.

strong.   Our data suggest, on the other hand, that this has not been due to any absence of offers of employment to the administrators.   These offers have come from a wide variety of professional institutions and private business firms.

Of the thirty-two who did not receive offers of employment from outside the government, many were emphatic in denying that they would ever receive such offers.   But this "civil-service mentality" is apparently not shared by many. Rather, the great majority stay in public employment because on the whole its incentives are satisfactory.   Many, to be sure, complain that government salaries are too low.   But the frequency of such complaints together with the ample opportunity to seek employment elsewhere does not seem to result in a rate of turnover at this level which is in excess of the turnover of professional employees in the P-1 classification.

Since this sample group was derived from the 1940 Official Register, the attempt was made to ascertain the employment status of the group at the end of 1945, the wartime experience of the group being left out of account.   In this manner it was possible to check the relative stability of the government service record of the group without taking the exceptional wartime conditions of government service into account.   Out of a total of 246 persons for whom data could be obtained, 55 had left Federal employment by the end of 1945 (or the beginning of 1946).   Another 18 had retired or died, and 25 had stayed in the government but had transferred to a different agency.   On the other hand, 149 out of 246, or 60.5 per cent, stayed in the departments in which they had worked in 1940 or returned to them after an interlude of wartime service elsewhere.[10]   The rate of turnover (that is, of separations) for the group as a whole was, therefore, 21.9 per cent.   This rate compared with a separation rate of 17.1 per cent for 1,920 P-1 appointees during 1935–1939.[11]

This result bears out the earlier finding of the Personnel Classification Board, according to which the rate of turnover in the higher professional grades is greater than in the lower grades.   It should be emphasized, on the other hand, that the separation rate for any group could be expected to be low during 1935–1939, when there was still widespread unemployment, as compared to 1945–46 with its manpower shortage in many fields.   While the findings of the Board are substantiated by these studies, the differences in stability between the different grades of the Federal service are not as great as is commonly believed.

It may be of interest also to observe what types of employment were taken up by the group of fifty-five respondents, most of whom had had prolonged experience

[10] If all cases are counted in which government service was continued after the war, including those who transferred to other agencies, the percentage of those who stayed increases to 70.5 per cent.   Of course, this reckoning leaves all deaths and retirements out of account.

[11] See Littlejohn, op. cit., p. 24.   The actual separation rate indicated by this study was 25 per cent.   This included, however, transfers to other government positions which amounted to 7.9 per cent (as compared with 10 per cent in our sample).

in the civil service, but who left it since 1940. How do these types of employment compare with their employment before entering the Federal service, and how do

TABLE XXVIII

Number of respondents leaving government service listed by periods during which they entered it

Period	Number
Before 1920	6
1920–1929	3
1930–1940	46
	55

TABLE XXIX

Percentage distribution of principal occupations of 55 respondents before and after government service as compared with the percentage distribution of job-offers received by 152 respondents

Occupations or type of business	Distribution of 55 respondents and of job-offers		
	Per cent distribution by occupation		Job-offers received by 152 respondents
	Before	After	
	Government service		
Farmer	3.7	2.0	0.2
Small business	9.0	—	40.3
Large business	5.4	14.0	
Government service (other than executive)	12.8	22.0	6.4
Professionals			
a. Lawyer	14.6	20.0	9.3
b. College teaching	16.3	9.0	14.1
c. Journalist	9.1	11.0	6.4
d. Other	16.3	—	20.1
Representative of private organization	—	22.0*	3.2*
Student	12.7	—	—
Total	100.0	100.0	100.0

* Of the respondents included in this item in the second column, seven became representatives of trade associations, two joined the CIO–PAC, two became associated with private research foundations, and one joined a private organization interested in housing. The composition of offers from private organizations is explained in the notes to Table XXVII, p. 64.

they compare with the employment opportunities of the group as a whole? These questions are answered by means of Tables XXVIII and XXIX.

These tables confirm that higher Federal employment is unstable among those who have entered it recently (particularly during the 1930's). This instability is reflected in the disproportionate number of younger persons (in terms of their service record) who leave the civil service rather than in their greater number of transfers while they are members of it (cf. Tables XXVI and XXVIII). The data presented in the last two tables suggest further that government service deflects those who leave it into types of employment which differ from their own former occupations. The percentage distribution of the jobs accepted by fifty-five respondents differs also from the distribution of job-offers which the group as a whole has received.[12] Offers of employment by law firms, trade associations, and other private organizations, other government agencies, newspapers, and to some extent business, were more readily taken up than similar offers coming from universities or other professional types of employment.[13] These data are insufficient. But this line of questioning may facilitate insights into the types of employment alternatives open to Federal administrators and the choices which government experience prompts them to make.

The preceding discussion raises a number of questions. Government needs more professionals, yet superior educational background is not readily rewarded. How will this discrepancy affect the relationship between education and public service? Our review of incentives suggested that by and large the civil service operates competitively in the labor market, succeeding in attracting those to whom it can offer higher salaries than their positions in private employment. Yet an account of comparative salaries in private and public employment does not probe the problem of their relative prestige. Nor does it answer the query how persons of the social characteristics which we have described operate in the "administrative climate," even if it does explain why they entered the Federal service. The data on the education and previous experience of administrators suggested that 1932 was a turning point in American public administration. But they do not reveal whether this development is to be understood in terms of a professionalization of the civil service. They do not reveal what changes are occurring in the culture-pattern of American Federal administration.

The preceding chapters describe the social characteristics of a group of higher Federal administrators. These data provide background information but by themselves do not give a clue to the manner in which these administrators exercise

---

[12] The latter comparison relates the types of employment taken up by 55 respondents who left the government to the job-offers received by 152. Obviously, the job-offers received by the 55 would be similar to or identical with the positions which they actually accepted. It is of interest, on the other hand, to observe the contrast between the percentage distribution of the jobs actually taken and the distribution of offers by types of employment which the group as a whole received. For a study in which the post-government jobs of a different group of administrators are analyzed, see E. P. Herring, *Federal Commissioners*, p. 135.

[13] This statement does not mean that these 55 persons chose these types of employment in preference to the others. It means rather that among all the offers received by 152 administrators certain offers of employment were more readily accepted. Thus the types of employment which the 55 took up after their government service are significant for the group as a whole.

their delegated authority. Yet the relation between policy-directives and policy-implementation has been the subject of many studies of administration. The large size, the detailed division of labor, and the specific enumeration of the duties of each position, which characterize modern large-scale organizations in industry and government, pose many technical problems for the administrator, who is concerned with the execution of policies. One of the most important of these problems lies in the fact that the major policies in business and government are formulated as general directives whose execution requires the exercise of administrative discretion. The remaining chapters of this study will be concerned with the social and psychological setting which affects this discretion in the case of high American administrators in the Federal civil service.[14] But first it will be useful to examine the literature which has dealt with this problem in its theoretical, historical, and social aspects.

[14] The studies of administrative discretion have so far not been concerned with this aspect but with the various rules and procedures by which administrative discretion is controlled. An exception is the study by Philip Selznic, *TVA and the Grass Roots* (Berkeley: University of California Press, 1949).

CHAPTER VII

THE STUDY OF BUREAUCRACY IN LARGE-SCALE ORGANIZATIONS*

Men have combined their efforts in large-scale organizations throughout history, but they have done so under many different circumstances, and their more or less voluntary cooperation has taken many different forms. The large-scale organizations of modern Western civilization are not noteworthy for their size but for the problems peculiar to our forms of organized cooperation. These forms are characteristically modern in so far as they depend on a minute division of labor and on the precise enumeration of rights and duties with which a person is endowed for the duration of his service. If such a specification of rights and duties is consistently carried out, it will result ideally in an exhaustive definition of the powers of command (their extent and their limits) appropriate to every position within an administrative hierarchy. However, we do not ordinarily think of large-scale organizations in this sense. We are rather inclined to note that their division of labor leads to red tape and to monotonous work for the individual employee; and we suspect, even if we may not be able to prove it, that especially the higher employees of such organizations will be able and eager to evade their duties and abuse their authority.

THE "IRON LAW OF OLIGARCHY"[1]

Many students of the role of large-scale organization in Western civilization take this latter view. They readily grant that our civilization could not survive without such organizations. Yet they assert that the policies of these organizations will in effect be determined by their organized minorities, for whom the unorganized membership is no match.[2] To these students it is consequently meaningless to distinguish between different organizations by the purposes they are said to serve. Rather, the interests of the ruling clique determine the purpose of any organization.

But can these interests or purposes be readily ascertained? The purpose of business organizations, for instance, is ordinarily termed profit-making. Yet, the individuals who conduct a business have a great diversity of interests in mind,

---

* This chapter was previously published in the *American Sociological Review*, XII (October, 1947), 493–501. It is here reprinted in substance with the permission of the Editor.

[1] The most comprehensive statement of this theory is contained in Robert Michels, *Political Parties* (New York: Hearst's International Library, 1919) and Gaetano Mosca, *The Ruling Class* (New York: McGraw-Hill Book Co. 1939). Cf. also the recent restatement of the theory by Philip Selznick, "An Approach to the Theory of Bureaucracy," *American Sociological Review*, VIII (1943), 47–59.

[2] Cf. Mosca, *op. cit.*, p. 53.

of which profit-making for the business may be one. The relation between the interests of individuals and the purpose of profit-making is indeterminate in the sense that any number of different administrative actions might lead to business success. Except as individual cases are examined empirically,[3] it is difficult, if not impossible, to determine in what manner the various interests of individuals have contributed towards the purpose (profit-making) of a business. It will be less ambiguous, then, if we speak of the success rather than the purpose of an organization, since we can do so without judging the intricate interrelations between administration and its results.

In pursuing their own interests the members of an organized minority may, however, prevent the success of an organization. This possibility may be attributed to the fact that the organized minority has formed an idea of the success of an organization which conflicts with the ideas which others have formed. The criteria of success are themselves controversial. Such controversy is likely to exist both inside and outside any large-scale organization. It is, therefore, misleading to assume that a ruling clique can deliberately prevent the success of an organization, while everybody else agrees on the methods and the desirability of achieving it. Rather, an organized minority can maintain its power and can make its idea of success prevail as long as disagreement is widespread both about the meaning of success and about the methods by which it is to be achieved.

The "iron law of oligarchy" is inadequate in that it speaks of the superior power of an organized minority without giving sufficient attention to the causes of *dissensus* inside and outside the organization which is studied. The "law" is also inadequate in so far as it is based on a narrow, technical view of administration. It assumes, along with the administrative technician, that the administrative process is both *rational* and *neutral*. As a result it asserts that an organized minority can use its position of power to direct an organization in accordance with the minority's interests. To this end the minority can count on the efficient and disinterested service of the employees of the organization. These assertions confuse, however, the *concept* of technically rational administration[4] with the *reality* of the administrative process. No large-scale organization is in fact technically rational, because it must always involve

a) the social and ideological background of a diversity of persons, which their formal positions within an administrative hierarchy cannot obliterate;

b) the institutional setting in which the organization must function and its effect on the psychology of its internal operation;

[3] For an illustration of the difficulties involved in ascertaining how decisions in business are arrived at, cf. the study by Robert A. Gordon, *Business Leadership in the Large Corporations* (Washington: Brookings-Institution, 1945), pp. 46–98. The same point is illustrated in Leo Tolstoy's characterization of the relation between General Staff decisions and actual military action. See *War and Peace* (New York: Modern Library, n.d.), pp. 1110–1146.

[4] This term refers to Max Weber's ideal type of modern administration. As pointed out earlier, the term refers to the professionalization of the civil service, indicating both the expert competence of the administrator and his strict adherence to the ideal of neutrality.

c) the historical and psychological context in which the people outside the organization view its activities.

It is the special task of the sociologist to observe the effects of this social context on the operation of an ideally rational administration. The social context, especially that of the higher Federal service in the United States, will be the subject of the next two chapters.

These considerations indicate that the power of any organized minority is circumscribed by the internal and external social setting of the large-scale organization, which it seeks to control. Such an organization can be used in the interest of a minority the more easily the more the administrators behave in a technically rational way; that is, the more the administrators hold to the ideal of impartial, competent service. But this ideal is perhaps never realized, since the actions leading to its realization cannot themselves (by definition) be motivated by the spirit of neutrality. If an organized minority will use an organization for its own interests, it must, therefore, resort frequently to the deliberate manipulation of personal and ideological influences. In this way it may undermine rather than foster the tendencies which might otherwise strengthen the technically rational aspects of administration. Perhaps the most telling illustration of this point is the experience of the German Secret Police, which had encouraged denunciations in order to facilitate the systematic detection of all latent opposition to the Hitler regime. This policy made it imperative from time to time to denounce the denouncers, because the flood of denunciations made for various personal reasons had become unmanageable.[5]

But if there is no regular connection between rational administration and oligarchical abuse, neither is there such a connection between rational administration and democratic institutions. Broadly speaking, whether one or the other will be the result, depends upon the social and psychological setting in which a technically rational administration is attempted. However, the students of large-scale organization have failed so far to make this dependence the center of their analyses. They have rather been concerned either with tracing the processes by which modern administration in business or government has become technically more rational or with analyzing the human factor, which is necessarily involved in large-scale organization.[6] Concentration on either one of these concerns has tended to obscure the real issue. Modern large-scale organizations do not show a clear separation of the technical and the psychological aspects. They may be more

---

[5] See E. Kohn-Bramstedt, *Dictatorship and Political Police* (London: Kegan Paul, 1945), pp. 114–115. If a dictatorial regime attempts to avoid this difficulty by discouraging denunciations, it usually finds itself compelled, in the absence of spontaneous information, to organize a system of spies upon spies. Such systematic efforts at obtaining needed information entails its own unforeseen consequences. How this system may affect factory production is illustrated by Victor Kravchenko, *I Chose Freedom* (New York: Charles Scribner's Sons, 1946), pp. 75–81.

[6] I leave out of consideration the voluminous literature on the art of management. Interestingly enough this literature also treats of the rational techniques of management (*e.g.*, testing, job classification, time- and motion-studies) separately from a psychological study of personnel and public relations.

readily understood, I believe, if the interrelations between the technical requirements of the flow of work and the social and psychological predispositions of the individuals engaged in this work are analyzed. Our understanding of this interrelation may be enhanced, however, by a brief examination of the studies in which these aspects have been treated of separately. This examination may be useful as an introduction to the theoretical analysis of this interrelation at the end of this chapter; in the next two chapters an attempt will be made at analyzing this interrelation empirically.

STUDIES OF RATIONALIZATION

It is a familiar idea that modern Western civilization is increasingly characterized by bureaucratization. In the past scientific analyses have characterized this development as one of increasing "rationalization." Applied to administration in the executive branch this term refers to the substitution of learnable rules of procedure for the exercise of individual caprice (of the king or his representatives). It also refers to the ascendance of a nation-wide administration of executive functions over the autonomy of small, decentralized government units with their adherence to local traditions. The German historian Otto Hintze has shown, for instance, how the modern cabinet system gradually developed out of the various offices in the king's household. He has traced the Treasury or Finance Department in various modern governments to the king's servant who was responsible for collecting and guarding the monies owed to the king. In addition, modern administration has clearly separated state from household finance and in so doing has replaced the traditional and erratic methods of the past by regularized and formally legal administrative procedures.[7] This same rationalization of government has been analyzed by Ernest Barker in his study of the development of public services in France, England, and Prussia since 1660.[8] Professor Barker has stated that prior to 1660 the state was still identified with the king's family household. Its resources were the king's private property and the nobility had special privileges in the government's administrative and military organization consisting of claims on offices and on the revenues obtained from them. He writes:

This confusion of the idea of the State with notions of Family, Property and general Society was generally characteristic of Europe about 1660. . . . So long as it persists, it complicates and checks the development of a pure and specific administration of public services. The disengaging of the idea of the State, as a service-rendering organization for the protection of rights and en-

[7] Otto Hintze, "Die Entstehung der modernen Staatsministerien," *Historische Zeitschrift*, C (1907), 60–64, 70–72, 91. See also T. F. Tout, "The English Civil Service in the 14th Century," in *Collected Papers* (Manchester: Manchester University Press, 1934), III, 191–221.

[8] Ernest Barker, *The Development of Public Services in Western Europe, 1660–1930* (New York: Oxford University Press, 1944).

forcement of duties, is the prior condition of such a development. There are two great land-marks in the history of that disengaging. One is the institution of absolutism, as it was inaugurated by Louis XIV. The other is the proclamation of national sovereignty, as it was made in 1789. Both of these movements, opposed as they are, agree in postulating a conception of the State as something separate and *sui generis*.[9]

Professor Barker has traced in some detail the history of this disengagement in the fields of administration, conscription, taxation, social services, and education. Barker's and Hintze's analyses indicate that administration in the modern state is by contrast clearly separate from the "general society," with which it was confused at an earlier time. Indeed, in analyzing the over-all result of the development, which these historians have traced, contemporary sociology has centered its attention on this disengagement of the administration of executive functions from society.

According to Max Weber the key to an understanding of modern administration lies in the concept of professionalization.[10] Specialized training and thorough examinations are today indispensable prerequisites for the recruitment of administrators. They are appointed rather than elected. Their work in its professional capacity is integrated into a hierarchy of command by way of enabling statutes and procedural rules. The special competence of each appointee is utilized in fulfilling the particular duties ascribed to the office which he (temporarily) occupies. As an ideal type, administration in the modern (as contrasted with feudal) forms of political organization is the very antithesis of arbitrary rule. Its every action is predictable, since the principles of its organization are designed to rule out any possible intrusion of personal factors, such as political convictions, personal bias, or corruption.

This construction of rational administration rests on the assumption that office holders as a group believe in this rationality. Rationalization of the administrative process depends on the development of a professional ethics. The administrator must be thoroughly committed to a faithful execution of his duties. He must be devoted to a preservation of the impersonal character of his work, and must confine it within the limits of his professional competence.[11] In return he will demand a regular salary, security of tenure, regularized advancement, and pension provisions. In addition, he ordinarily expects that his position as an agent of the government carries a reasonable degree of social prestige, the more so since his

---

[9] *Ibid.*, pp. 5–6. (Reprinted here by permission of the publisher.)

[10] Cf. for the following discussion the chapter on bureaucracy in H. H. Gerth and C. Wright Mills, *From Max Weber: Essays in Sociology*, pp. 196–244.

[11] This last maxim of his professional ethic is usually formulated in terms of the distinction between routine administration and the political process. Cf. Karl Mannheim, *Ideology and Utopia* (New York: Harcourt, Brace and Co., 1936), pp. 100–103, and Ramsay Muir, *Peers and Bureaucrats* (London: Constable, 1910), pp. 31 and 37. See also in this connection Alfred Weber's characterization of national differences in the professional ethics of administrators in his essay, "Der Beamte," in *Ideen zur Staats- und Kultur-soziologie* (Karlsruhe: G. Braun, 1927), pp. 88–101.

educational training and his standing as a technical expert should bring such esteem regardless of the public office which he occupies.

These studies of rationalization in the administration of executive functions have in common an emphasis on the differences between administration in the modern state and administration under feudalism and other forms of political organization. Modern public administration is more rational than administration under feudalism or in the era of absolute monarchies because it seeks to minimize tradition and the identification of office and incumbent. The performance of given tasks in modern administration has become more uniform and predictable for these reasons. But it does not follow that this performance is *in fact* uniform and predictable. For, as has been shown in many recent studies,[12] the greater rationality of modern organizations has failed to eliminate the human factor. This factor has not been ignored by the scholars who have emphasized the development of rationalization; many of them have in fact analyzed the various consequences which this rationalization has entailed.[13]

Men are unable and unwilling to restrain the further development of technology and administrative organization. At the same time they cannot utilize the products of their efforts for their own increased material, cultural, and psychological well-being. The various implications of this problem have been one of the major concerns of modern sociology. Karl Marx observed[14] that the machine had become the embodiment of man's intellect and had atrophied the human faculties of the worker. Toennies and Simmel[15] emphasized that the substitution of the rational cash-nexus for the more personal relationships of an earlier society brought in its wake the dissolution of traditional social bonds and threatened the very rationality of modern society. Finally, Mannheim has shown[16] that modern technological and administrative organizations involved a disjunction between substantial and functional rationality. That is to say, persons employed in modern occupations are divided into two classes—namely, those competent to construct the blueprints of technical apparatus or administrative organization and those competent to read and apply these blueprints without being able to comprehend the principles on which they are based.

The more complicated technology and administration become, the more difficult

---

[12] See below for a discussion of some of these studies.

[13] Cf., among others, W. F. Ogburn, *Social Change* (New York: Viking Press, 1922) in the field of technology; E. Rothschild, *The Meaning of Unintelligibility in Modern Art* (Chicago: University of Chicago Press, 1934) for art; and Robert Redfield, *The Folkculture of Yucatan* (Chicago: University of Chicago Press, 1941) in relation to city life.

[14] Karl Marx, *Capital* (New York: The Modern Library, 1936), 395–404. See also Thomas Carlyle, *Past and Present* (New York: Mershon Co., n.d.), p. 9: "Things, if it be not mere cotton and iron things, are growing disobedient to man."

[15] Ferdinand Toennies, *Gemeinschaft und Gesellschaft* (Leipzig: Hans Buske, 1935), pp. 8–86 and Georg Simmel, *Philosophie des Geldes* (Leipzig: Duncker & Humblot, 1910), Ch. V.

[16] Karl Mannheim, *Man and Society in an Age of Reconstruction* (New York: Harcourt, Brace and Co., 1941), pp. 39–75.

it also becomes to control the uses to which these tools are put. Indeed, the increasing size of the organizations in industry and government may lead to an increasing desire to escape from the necessity of deliberation and rational calculation.[17] This desire will in turn increase man's disability to control the products of his scientific and organizational enterprises. The human factor is indeed considered by those who emphasize the development of rationalization, but it is considered in terms of the effects of this development. However, the human factor has not been considered as a contemporary and indispensable foundation[18] on which the rationality of business and of public administration depends. It is, for example, insufficient to state that the efficiency of public administration depends upon the professionalization of its officials. What factors promote or retard this professionalization? It is true that administration becomes more uniform and predictable if the people who are affected will respect the administrator for the neutrality with which he performs his duties. But what fosters this attitude of respect? Furthermore, it is true that rational administration depends on the ability of administrators to encourage cooperation and initiative in their subordinates. But what are the conditions which favor the development of such abilities? Obviously it is insufficient to characterize only the formal prerequisites of administrative rationalization; it is necessary to consider its human preconditions as well.[19]

STUDIES OF THE HUMAN FACTOR

To the extent that students of government administration have considered these human preconditions at all, they have taken their cue from various analyses of industrial organization. Although many differences exist between industry and government, the problems of administration are sufficiently alike to make the studies of one type of organization useful for an understanding of the other. It is for this reason that I turn to a brief consideration of industrial relations.

The students of rationalization in industry have emphasized from the first that it is important to consider the individual participant in the production process. For instance, historians concerned with the rise of the modern factory have stressed the traditional working habits and the lack of accuracy and discipline which stood in the way of this development. In the words of the Hammonds:

Scarcely any evil associated with the factory system was entirely a new evil in kind. In many domestic industries the hours were long, the pay was poor, the children worked from a

---

[17] Cf. on this point Erich Fromm, *Escape from Freedom* (New York: Farrar and Rinehart, 1941), pp. 24–39, 103–35.

[18] As distinguished from its consideration in an analysis of the history of modern rationalization.

[19] It may be objected that these are considered, for example, in the various studies of personnel management. However, these studies, important as they are, are practical, not analytic; they fail to probe the conditions which spell the success or failure of their practical application. A provocative analysis of this problem is contained in Herbert A. Simon, "The Proverbs of Administration," *Public Administration Review*, VI (1946), 53–67. See also by the same author, *Administrative Behavior* (New York: The Macmillan Co., 1948).

tender age, there was over-crowding. . . . But the home worker at the worst . . . was in many respects his own master. He worked long hours, but they were his own hours; his wife and children worked, but they worked beside him, and there was no alien power over their lives. . . . The forces that ruled his fate were in a sense outside his daily life; they did not overshadow and envelop his home, his family, his movements and habits. . . .

What the new order did in all these respects was to turn the discomforts of the life of the poor into a rigid system. . . . To all the evils from which the domestic worker had suffered, the Industrial Revolution added discipline, and the discipline of a power driven by a competition that seemed as inhuman as the machines that thundered in factory and shed.[20]

Clearly, this process entailed untold suffering. But many of the historians from Marx to the Hammonds viewed this human aspect of the industrial revolution primarily in ethical terms. They failed to take fully into account the fact that the suffering which occurred during the Industrial Revolution was the instrument by which the human material was gradually shaped into conformity with the requirements of machine production.[21]

This humanitarian concern with the human factor (during the period of industrialization) was a response to management's attitude towards the worker. Nevertheless, that attitude determined the early organization of the production process. In writing of this problem as it appeared during the early 19th century, the Hammonds have shown by what reasoning the absolute supremacy of the *entrepreneur* was justified. It suffices to quote one of the arguments which were popular at the time:

When there is too much labor in the market and wages are too low, do not combine to raise the wages; do not combine in the vain hope of compelling the employer to pay more for labor than there are funds for the maintenance of labor; but go out of the market. Leave the relations between wages and labor to equalize themselves. You can never be permanently kept down in wages by the profits of capital; for if the profits of capital are too high, the competition of other capital immediately comes in to set the matter right.[22]

"It is easy to see," say the Hammonds by way of comment, "how this kind of reasoning produced the prevalent view of the capitalist as beneficent whatever the wages he paid or the conditions he imposed."[23] Yet, ironically, these very practices of exploitation had eventually the effect of decreasing rather than increasing industrial production. Indeed, scientific management began with the discovery that exploitation led to lower productive output.

Years ago Robert Owen wrote as follows:

Many have long experienced in manufacturing operations the advantages of substantial, well-contrived, and well-executed machinery. Experience has also shown the difference of the

[20] J. L. and Barbara Hammond, *The Town Laborer, 1760–1832* (London: Longmans, Green and Co., 1925), pp. 18–19. (Reprinted here by permission of the publisher.)

[21] Contemporary illustrations of the importance of this factor may be found in John Scott, *Behind the Urals* (Boston: Houghton Mifflin Co., 1942) and Kuo-Heng Shih, *China Enters the Machine Age* (Cambridge: Harvard University Press, 1944).

[22] Quoted in Hammond, *op. cit.*, p. 209. (Reprinted here by permission of the publisher.)

[23] *Ibid.*

results between mechanism which is neat, clean, well-arranged, and always in a high state of repair; and that which is allowed to be dirty, in disorder . . . and much out of repair.

If then, due care as to the state of inanimate machines can produce such beneficial results, what may not be expected if you devote equal attention to your vital machines, which are far more wonderfully constructed?

And in answering the question which he had posed, Robert Owen indicated that it was *profitable* to consider the role of the human factor in the production process. He writes further:

I have expended much time and capital upon improvements of the living machinery; and it will soon appear that the time and money so expended in the manufactory of New Lanark, even while such improvements are in progress only, and but half of their beneficial effects attained, are now producing a return exceeding 50%, and will shortly create profits equal to cent per cent on the original capital expended in them.[24]

From Owen's day to the recent development of industrial sociology it has been a recurrent theme that proper and controlled attention to the worker's subjective role in the production process would be both humanitarian and advantageous. Although Owen was a reformer and stressed the financial advantage for propagandistic reasons, later writers retained this appeal primarily because empirical studies showed the positive effect of improved personnel policies on individual output. Frederick Taylor's statement of this idea may serve as an illustration:

The majority of men believe that the fundamental interests of employees and employers are necessarily antagonistic. Scientific management, on the contrary, has for its very foundation the firm conviction that the true interests of the two are one and the same; that prosperity of the employer cannot exist through a long term of years unless it is accompanied by prosperity for the employee, and vice versa; and that it is possible to give the workman what he most wants— high wages—and the employer what he wants—a low labor cost—for his manufacture.[25]

It should be remembered that Taylor confined himself to considerations of human efficiency. He was concerned with substituting a rigorously-planned working performance for the traditional, rule-of-thumb approach of each employee to his work. Taylor believed that his goals (as defined above) could be attained by detailed time- and motion-studies. But his writings show that he was aware of the many psychological problems which stood in the way of getting his scheme of "task management" accepted by the worker and by management.

Taylor's successors have become increasingly concerned with the psychological problems which are incident to the rationalization of the production process.

---

[4] Robert Owen, *The Formation of Character* (1813) quoted in L. Urwick and E. F. L. Brech, *The Making of Scientific Management* (London: Management Publication Trust, 1946), II, p. 57. The authors of this work ask: "If the principles of effective management were understood, why was it that hours of work were universally so long and conditions so poor? Why did Owen encounter such opposition in his fight for minimum standards laid down by law?" (*Ibid.*, p. 66.) The answer does not simply lie in a reference to the forces of competition or the bigotry and ignorance of the employers, though both undoubtedly were of importance. As mentioned above, considerable importance should be attributed to the tradition of compulsion, which the enforcement of a new work-discipline initiated, because it was indispensable in machine production.

[25] Frederick W. Taylor, *The Principles of Scientific Management* (New York: Harper and Brothers, 1919), p. 10. (Reprinted here by permission of the publisher.)

They have continued the experimental testing of various factors which were either positively or negatively correlated with the output of the individual worker. This experimentation has indicated that the factors constituting the external working conditions are neither singly nor in combination responsible for the changes in the output of the individual worker so long as they are considered apart from the social and psychological effects of his status in the work-group.[26]

The famous Hawthorne experiments[27] confirm this point. Controlled observation of small work-groups over a number of years indicated that increased production on the whole seemed more closely related to the morale of the group than to any of the variables (such as differently spaced rest pauses, mid-morning meals, higher pay, variations in illumination, temperature, and so on) which were tested.[28] Morale was related, on the other hand, to the improved supervision, the prestige position of each member of the test-group and the increased attention which individual problems, opinions, and suggestions received.

This result of the experiments was regarded as a discovery for two reasons. The history of the labor movement and of labor legislation had focused attention on the attainment of minimal working conditions (such as hours, wages, safety devices). This made it appear plausible that these conditions of work were the causes of satisfaction. Moreover, managers have traditionally thought of the worker as a subordinate antagonist whose every demand was a challenge to their authority. That attitude militated against any concern with the causes of dissatisfaction. Despite the fact that many have regarded the Hawthorne experiments as discoveries, they actually have only confirmed an old insight. For example, Robert Owen was aware of the fact that the worker's satisfaction and full cooperation in the production process depended upon his recognition as a responsible human being and could not be obtained as long as he was treated as a cog in the production process. And Karl Marx discerned the human problem of industrial civilization when he pointed out that the cooperation of laborers was not the result of their own efforts, but instead the work of an "alien power" over them. He writes:

Laborers (under capitalism) cannot cooperate without being brought together: their assemblage in one place is a necessary condition of their cooperation. . . . Being independent of each other, the laborers are *isolated persons* who enter into relations with the capitalist, but not

---

[26] Elton Mayo, *The Human Problems of an Industrial Civilization* (Boston: Harvard University, Graduate School of Business Administration, 1946), pp. 1–54.

[27] In addition to the writings of Elton Mayo cf. especially F. J. Roethlisberger and W. J. Dickson, *Management and the Worker* (Cambridge: Harvard University Press, 1943) and T. N. Whitehead, *Leadership in a Free Society* (Cambridge: Harvard University Press, 1936) and the same author's *The Industrial Worker* (Cambridge: Harvard University Press, 1938) 2 vols.

[28] This statement disregards the relatively few cases in which personal preoccupation interfered with the workers output. Cf. Mayo, *op. cit.*, pp. 101–112.

with one another. This cooperation begins only with the labor process, *but they have then ceased to belong to themselves.* On entering that process they become incorporated with capital.[29]

And somewhat further on in his analysis Marx speaks of the human consequences of this mediated cooperation of the workers as follows:

While simple cooperation leaves the mode of working by the individual unchanged, manufacture thoroughly revolutionises it. . . . It converts the laborer into a crippled monstrosity, by forcing his detail dexterity at the expense of a world of productive capabilities and instincts. . . . The knowledge, the judgment and the will, which, though in ever so small a degree, are practised by the independent peasant and handicraftsman . . . these faculties are now required only for the workshop as a whole. Intelligence in production expands in one direction, because it vanishes in many others. What is lost by the detail laborers, is concentrated in the capital that employs them. It is a result of the division of labor in manufactures, that the laborer is brought face to face with the intellectual potencies of the material process of production as the property of another, and as a ruling power.[30]

It is consistent with this statement to say that real human satisfaction is not to be found in the various improvements of working conditions, important though they are. And these insights of nearly a century ago are again confirmed by the statement that many conflicting forces and attitudes, which are found in industrial relations,

center about . . . the work and the manner of its performance. Somehow or other, no effective relationship between the "worker and his work" had been established; and since a community of interests at this point was lacking the group failed to establish an integrate activity and fell into a degree of discord which no one could understand or control. . . . If an individual cannot work with sufficient understanding of his work situation, then, unlike a machine, he can only work against opposition from himself.[31]

By what factors, then, is the development of morale and cooperation among workers hampered? As is well known, Marx did not believe that it was possible to incorporate the worker's initiative, pride, and whole-hearted cooperation in a common task of production. That possibility did not exist as long as the worker was subject to the compulsions of an organization whose operation and purpose were planned and conducted without his participation. On the other hand, it seems to be the contention of the various authors associated with the Industrial Research of the Harvard School of Business that Management is in a position to create the conditions under which this morale, this spirit of cooperation on the part of the workers can flourish. F. J. Roethlisberger writes as follows:

Maintaining internal equilibrium within the social organization of the plant involves keeping the channels of communication free and clear so that orders are transmitted downward without

[29] Karl Marx, *op. cit.*, pp. 361 and 365. (This and the following quotations are reprinted here by permission of Charles H. Kerr and Co. Supplement and italics mine.)
[30] *Ibid.*, pp. 396–397.
[31] Mayo, *op. cit.*, pp. 118–119, (Reprinted here by permission of the publisher.)

distortion and so that relevant information regarding situations at the work level is transmitted upward without distortion to those levels at which it can be best made use of. This involves getting the bottom of the organization to understand the economic objectives of the top; it also means getting the top of the organization to understand the feelings and sentiments of the bottom.[32]

But the policy which is advocated here does not seem feasible in the light of the experimental evidence on which it is based.

The so-called Relay Assembly Test Group, to give but one example, (this group of five girls was carefully observed for a number of years) showed a great deal of cooperation with the experimenters and among themselves with the result that their level of output increased considerably. But this cooperation was due to the considered attention bestowed on the group rather than to its external working conditions. Such detailed attention to the individual worker is incompatible with a large-scale production process. Mr. Roethlisberger says further:

> To the investigators, it was essential that the workers give their full and whole-hearted cooperation to the experiment. . . . In order to bring this about, the investigators did everything in their power to secure the complete cooperation of their subjects, *with the result that almost all the practices common to the shop were altered.*[33]

He himself concludes, therefore, that under the working conditions of large-scale production it is impossible to provide a setting which promotes a cooperation equal to that of the experimental group.[34] Nevertheless, the experimenters proceeded to develop an interview program which was designed to free the production process from the various emotional difficulties and personal antagonisms that lowered the output of some of the workers under observation. But such interviews could not reproduce under ordinary working conditions what the experiment had achieved—namely, to give each person pride in his work and in the successful performance of the group. The interviews, when practiced at large, could only succeed in eliminating from the production process the various personal factors which had so far persistently retarded its further rationalization. On balance it proved to be more efficient to have the individual worker unburden his personal troubles to an interviewer, even if that cut down his time on the job; he was not a good worker while he worried about personal affairs, and he was likely to slow up his fellow-workers. The cooperation of the workers was not increased, but some human obstacle to the further rationalization of the production process was eliminated.

[32] Reprinted by permission of the publishers from Fritz Jules Roethlisberger, *Management and Morale* (Cambridge, Mass.: Harvard University Press, 1941), pp. 192–193.

[33] Reprinted by permission of the publishers from Fritz Jules Roethlisberger, *Management and Morale* (Cambridge, Mass.: Harvard University Press, 1941), p. 14. (Italics mine.)

[34] See also Whitehead, *Industrial Worker*, I, p. 254.

I have tried to indicate in what manner the psychological problems arising out of rationalization in industry have been analyzed. The basic shortcoming of these studies is that their authors fail to show a sufficient awareness of the technological and institutional compulsions of large-scale organizations. Mayo, Roethlisberger, and others have assumed that the production goals set by management furnish the only valid criteria for the interpretation and evaluation of industrial relations.[35] As a result they have found that workers are insufficiently cooperative, although they attribute this attitude to the ills of our civilization.[36] But what appears as insufficient cooperation from the managerial point of view may be evidence of cooperation nevertheless. It is found, for example, that workers tend to set social standards for the output of their group through informal understandings. Does this mean that they lack the spirit of cooperation, or that their spirit differs from that desired by the employer? Roethlisberger has stated that such behavior is evidence of the "lack of social function" in the job of the worker.[37] But can improved personnel policies restore to the worker that feeling of personal importance and integrity which the production process denies him? Is such a personnel policy even compatible with the organizational requirements of the production process? Mayo and others have stated that in our society "collaboration cannot be left to chance."[38] They believe that the suspicion, hostility, and conflict which beset our industrial world, can be at least greatly alleviated if management sees its way towards improving employee relations. But they fail to ask how much the good morale of workers is worth in monetary terms and are indifferent to the question whether the process of production generates the very hostilities which interfere with its operation.[39]

THE PROBLEM OF BUREAUCRACY

The analysis of large-scale organization in the modern world will be deficient as long as analysts make either the formal structure or the informal human relations within that structure the vantage point of their observations. In the historical approach modern organization in industry or government is conceived in terms of a contrast with earlier forms. Consequently, it stresses the greater rationality of modern organization. In the managerial approach, on the other hand, attention is focussed on the as yet unmanaged aspect of human relations, which have asserted themselves in all organizations. The tacit assumption is

---

[35] Cf. Burleigh B. Gardner, *Human Relations in Industry* (Chicago: Richard D. Irwin, 1945), who defines the factory as "a coordinated system of activities directed to the production of goods," (p. 4).

[36] Elton Mayo, *The Social Problems of an Industrial Civilization* (Cambridge: Harvard University Press, 1945), ch. I.

[37] Roethlisberger, *Management and Morale*, pp. 24–25.

[38] Elton Mayo's Foreword to Roethlisberger, *Management and Morale*, p. xix.

[39] As a result industrial problems are almost exclusively treated as problems of defective communication. Cf. Gardner, *op. cit., passim.*

made that thorough study will show us how these "remaining human irrationalities" may become manageable. But this assumption is unwarranted in so far as the division of labor and the work-relations requisite for the organization of production (or of public administration) necessitate precisely those irrationalities which management is now seeking to remove.

A sufficient theoretical basis for the study of bureaucracy cannot be established by the observation that the students of rationalization overlook the human factor and that the students of human relations in industry neglect its formal structure. Instead, it is necessary to show in what manner all large-scale organizations require for their success a proper irrational foundation of the formal rules which are designed to govern day-to-day operations. In this respect the basic problem is the same throughout. The administration of a business or an executive agency of government depends for its effectiveness on a clearly understood hierarchy of authority. Yet it would break down if every employee were to follow all regulations to the letter and consult his superior whenever these rules do not provide sufficient guidance. Such typically bureaucratic behavior would interfere with the functioning of an organization at every point. Administration depends, on the other hand, on the ability and the willingness of employees to act on their own initiative. Yet it would be incompatible with effective operation if every official conducted the business assigned to him in accordance with his independent judgment. It is consequently imperative that the employees of all ranks in industry and government strike a balance between compliance and initiative, that they temper their adherence to formal rules by a judicious exercise of independent judgment, and that they fit their initiative into the framework of formal regulation. Both the effective exercise of power and the effective organization of production depend in some measure on this mixture of compliance with authority and the creative exercise of initiative. All large-scale organizations face the problem of finding formal and informal ways by which such a balance may be facilitated.

In stating the problem of bureaucracy in this manner we may have a clue to the systematic analysis and differentiation of large-scale organizations, which goes beyond the obvious contrast of government and business.[40] Attitudes toward risk-taking, toward authority, toward the public, as well as the institutional conditions of the "working climate," vary from country to country in both industry and government. These and other variables affect the relationship of the individual employee to the organizational hierarchy. They modify the manner in which an employee views his work within the organization and in relation to its

---

[40] In the study of business organizations it has always been assumed that they are essentially similar in countries of comparable economic structure. Certainly, the similarity of technical and administrative problems in large-scale industries makes this view plausible. Yet there is reason to believe that this assumption is misleading. Cf. the interesting essay by Herman Levy, *Volkscharakter und Wirtschaft*.

over-all purpose.   It may be useful to illustrate these points by contrasting the ideal types of democratic and authoritarian administration.[41]

Authoritarian administration is characterized by the fact that the official is both obedient and arbitrary.   His strict compliance with the orders of his superior is not tempered (as it is under democratic conditions) by responsiveness to public demands.[42]   Reliance is placed on the feeling of loyalty, which the official demonstrates by his unquestioning support of the prevailing order of authority.   Such loyalty implies a difference in status between officialdom and the public and in this manner testifies to the reliability of the authoritarian official.   In the execution of his orders the subordinate becomes a superior in his own right.   He acts as a leader to whose guidance the people should submit without question.   To be sure, his authority is limited, but the official nevertheless confronts his "public" as the representative of higher authority rather than as a public employee.

Several years ago two German writers made the following statement:

The official in the middle and the lower ranks of the service is in some respects similar to the officer. . . . Even without uniform there is a strong feeling of comradeship and a feeling of solidarity against civilians. . . . The subordination of lower to higher ranks in the officialdom is similar to relations in the army, and it is tolerable only when it is compensated for by a feeling of special status of the officials as against the public. . . . Officials in the middle and lower ranks still represent the superior power and wisdom of the state towards a public to whom the larger meaning of public administration is indifferent or incomprehensible.   Indeed, the official will tend to regard the importance of his administrative section the more highly the less he is able to comprehend the real over-all significance of his own work.[43]

In this as in all systems of administration much is left to the discretionary exercise of authority.   It lies in the spirit of authoritarian discretion that a successful maintenance of authority is in the end more important than its possible abuse. In case of failure the official is punished, not for an abuse of his authority, but for his "demonstrably disloyal" (that is, unsuccessful) exercise of it.   Such methods of administration lead in the extreme case to continuous suspicion downwards and the attempt to evade responsibility on the part of subordinates.   There is a

---

[41] Although this contrast is based on illustrations from government administration only, it applies equally well in my opinion to other types of large-scale organization.

[42] Authoritarian doctrine emphasizes that this unresponsiveness to public demands is itself in accord with the desires of the masses.   The prople want to be led and only the leaders are able to define the goals of political action and organize the people for their realization.   Authoritarian rule is justified on the ground that this rule truly represents the will of the people.

[43] Ottoheinz von der Gablentz and Carl Mennicke, *Deutsche Berufskunde*, (Leipzig: Bibliographisches Institut, 1930), pp. 428–429.   (My translation.)

telling description of this in Walter L. Dorn's analysis of Prussian bureaucracy under Frederick the Great:

> Frederick the Great cherished the inveterate belief that his officials were bent on deceiving him. . . . This distrust became an integral part of the bureaucratic system. Unreserved confidence he reposed in none of his ministers. He kept them in a perpetual state of uncertainty as to what he thought of their honesty and capacity. . . . He frequently struck upon the expedient of committing the task of reporting on any particular piece of business to two or three different officials, none of whom was aware that others were engaged in the same mission. When he did not wholly trust an official he charged an underling with secret supervision. To control his ministers he regularly corresponded with the presidents of the provincial chambers, and to assure himself of the veracity of the latter he often dealt with the individual members of the provincial chambers. By this continuous correspondence with officials and their subordinates, by controlling ministers through their subalterns and subordinates through their equals, the king tapped extraordinary sources of information which, besides the ordinary channels of information . . . , acquainted him with everything he seriously desired to know.[44]

Obviously, this system of authoritarian supervision has since become impractical with the growing complexity of administration in a modern state. Modern dictators have instituted instead elaborate administrative organizations for the systematic supervision of the political loyalty of the people and all government employees. A modern police system can employ the most advanced techniques in its closely calculated control of large populations.[45] Although these techniques have freed authoritarian supervision from the limitations of centralizing power in one person, they cannot escape from the continual duplication of their own supervisory checks, because no one spy can be trusted.

In democratic administration the execution of policy directives is subject to a more diffuse supervision than under authoritarian conditions. The democratic official is ideally expected to be obedient to his superior, but that obedience does not express at the same time his loyalty to the people's mandate. He is to exercise his authority in a spirit of service which does not require the unquestioning submission of the people for its realization. The democratic administrator stands, therefore, in an ambivalent relationship to his superior and his subordinate. His compliance, his orders, and his initiative are tempered by his anticipation of various public demands and by a sense of direct, if imponderable, accountability to the people. In this respect, superior and subordinate are equals before the public, although they are unequal within the administrative hierarchy. This peculiar

[44] Walter L. Dorn, "The Prussian Bureaucracy in the 18th Century," *Political Science Quarterly*, XLVI (September, 1931), 421–422. (Reprinted here by permission of the Managing Editor.) For a modern parallel see Alexander Barmine, *One Who Survived* (New York: G. P. Putnam's Sons, 1945), pp. 196–233, 237–245. A comparable situation in business is discussed in "The Stewardship of Sewell Avery," *Fortune*, XXXIII (May, 1946), 111–113, 179–186.

[45] This point is especially emphasized by E. Kohn-Bramstedt, *op. cit.*, pp. 2–6, 95–117, 137–156.

characteristic of democratic administration is well illustrated by the following statement of problems encountered in law enforcement:

> The policeman may observe a multitude of violations, some relating to laws and ordinances which were never intended by the enactors to be enforced, others involving minor regulations of public order.... Their very number and variety are such that their requirements are largely unknown to the people to whom they apply. Hence violations are extremely common....
>
> The policeman's art, then, consists in applying and enforcing a multitude of laws and ordinances in such degree or proportion and in such manner that the greatest degree of social protection will be secured. The degree of enforcement and the method of application will vary with each neighborhood and community. There are no set rules, nor even general guides to policy, in this regard. Each policeman must, in a sense, determine the standard which is to be set in the area for which he is responsible.... Thus he is a policy-forming police administrator in miniature, who operates beyond the scope of the usual devices of popular control. He makes and unmakes the fortunes of governmental executives and administrators, though rarely falling under the direct influence of the popular will. The only control to which he is subject is the discipline of his superiors.[46]

And yet his superiors are dependent for their success on the wisdom with which the policeman in his law-enforcement practices will respond to the indirect influences of the community.

In exercising such discretion in his direct contact with the public the democratic administrator is ideally concerned as much with the administering of a policy as with the execution of a command. (Indeed, he is always contributing to a policy, whether he knows it or not.) Yet this policy continues to be subject to a multiplicity of influences to which the administrator must remain sensitive. (Shifts in policy under authoritarian conditions always take the form of new orders from superiors.) This fact implies that the democratic official does his duty in the continuous anticipation of checks on his authority, both from his superior and from his "public" (for example, legislatures, pressure groups, and affected individuals.) He is trained to consider his office as a mandate of responsibilities, which are subject to more or less continuous modification. Yet his mandate is of a general character; it is meant to be an integral part of a scheme of policies in process of reformulation. He must, therefore, seek to re-define his function in this scheme on the presupposition that some specific policy emerges from the conflict of interests and in the belief that, whatever the policy, this conflict itself is a basic and worthwhile feature of the democratic process.

The authoritarian administrator is, on the other hand, more immune; his work is less directly subject to pressures from outside the official hierarchy. Under authoritarian conditions obedience and loyalty are synonymous, since each ad-

---

[46] Bruce Smith, *Police Systems in the United States* (New York: Harper and Brothers, 1940), p. 20. (Reprinted here by permission of the publisher.)

ministrative superior is ideally the only source of command, the representative
of the regime and the source of its policy formulation.   For each subordinate
policy emanates from the top and is unaffected by the administrator's direct contact with the public, although public reactions are certainly taken into account.
The role of each official in the execution of over-all policy is, consequently, a matter
of intra-administrative discussion and adjustment.   And because each subordinate administrator is in this sense remote from the public, responsibility for policy
determination is more clearly confined to the top administrators and is by the
same token less affected by public opinion.   It follows from these considerations
that an administration will be the more democratic the more its officials are directly
affected by the "antagonism of influences" and the more they are, therefore, drawn
into participating, more or less directly, in the processes of policy formation.

The preceding confrontation of two ideal types of bureaucracy may dispel some
misconception and focus attention on the major area of inquiry in this field.   Both
forms of administration may function efficiently.   This is the case under authoritarian conditions when the *esprit de corps* of the administrative group is high, its
loyalty to the regime intact and in harmony with public attitude, and its resultant
feeling of security a good foundation for the exercise of individual initiative.   It
is the case under democratic conditions when the spirit of public service among
administrators is well developed, their responsiveness to public demands kept
within limits by the public's restraint in pressing for individual privileges, and by
the administration's success in achieving consistent policy formulations which
represent genuine compromises of the various conflicting groups.

Both forms of bureaucracy may also develop the pathology of large-scale organizations.   Authoritarian bureaucracy can become a clique ridden by suspicion.
Its primary concern with self-preservation may result in the alienation of the
public, a growing inability to operate efficiently, and the duplication of functions,
which a more or less developed internal spy system necessitates.   Democratic
administration may deteriorate, on the other hand, because the frustrations of
administrative work deter qualified men and because suspicion of any authority
goes so far as to make effective policy formulation and execution impossible.

The temptation is strong to summarize the difference between democratic and
authoritarian administration by reference to Mannheim's distinction between
functional and substantial rationality.   Authoritarian officials would be thought
of as efficient in the use of administrative techniques without proper comprehension of their role in the over-all policy decided on by the dictator (functional rationality).   Democratic officials would combine, on the other hand, administrative efficiency with an understanding of the basic policies which they are called

upon to implement (substantial rationality).[47]   This application of Mannheim's distinction does not aid us, however, in our analysis of large-scale organizations. Mannheim himself would point out that all subordinate administrators suffer from the special incapacity which exclusive attention to the techniques of implementation entails.   Democratic and authoritarian officials share in the inability of comprehending the political program which governs their actions.   Besides, Mannheim's distinction suffers from overstating its case.[48]   It is impossible to run any large-scale organization without some provision for fitting the specialized technician into the larger framework of operation.   It is not possible, however, to direct his every action; some reliance must, therefore, be placed on his own over-all comprehension of his function and on the initiative which he develops in implementing this comprehension by cooperative action.   Thus both democratic and authoritarian officials must grapple with the problem of overcoming the "trained incapacity" (Veblen) of the administrative technician to see the larger policy framework.[49]

Democratic and authoritarian administrations differ, therefore, because of their respective institutions and culture-patterns, not because one is representative and inefficient, whereas the other is efficient but arbitrary.   The distinction between these two types of administration is rather an outgrowth of historical experience and present circumstances.   As such it affects the manner of the administrative technician, who combines obedience and efficiency with the initiative that is essential to the success of large-scale organization.   It is not useful, therefore, to consider the social problems of administration in terms either of rational management or of the psychology of human relations.   The problem of bureaucracy is rather in what manner technical and administrative rationality are combined with the exercise of individual initiative in the accomplishment of a common task.   Men have combined their efforts in large-scale organizations throughout history. Their success today will depend on whether or not they can combine the efficiency of modern organization with a flexibility which allows the individual in that organization to use his imagination rather than do his job in a routine way.

The problem of bureaucracy is, then, not only a question of preserving freedom against the encroachments of government.   Rather, we will not be able to utilize

---

[47] Indeed, this distinction has been used to characterize Nazi administration. See E. Kohn-Bramstedt, *op. cit.*, pp. 2–6 and John H. Herz "German Administration under the Nazi Regime," *American Political Science Review*, XL (August, 1946), 684–86.

[48] Karl Mannheim, *Man and Society*, pp.51–60,   It is not denied, of course, that Mannheim has pointed to a constant source of friction.   The distinction goes back to Karl Marx, *op. cit.*, pp. 361–365, 395–399.

[49] Both will tend to use the rationalizations of their respective political philosophies, for instance, as guidance in all cases in which they need but cannot obtain a knowledge of basic policies.   The behavioristic importance of political philosophies in a study of administrative conduct has not so far been sufficiently considered. See in this respect John M. Gaus, Leonard D. White, and Marshall E. Dimock, *The Frontiers of Public Administration* (Chicago: University of Chicago Press, 1936).

the efficiency of modern management unless we can make the initiative of the individual one of our principles of organization.   Our success in this respect depends in large part on the psychological and institutional assets and liabilities which are the warp and woof of public administration in the United States and in the other Western countries.   In the next two chapters I have attempted to outline some of these assets and liabilities pertaining to the administration of the Federal executive in the United States.

CHAPTER VIII

IS THERE A BUREAUCRATIC CULTURE-PATTERN IN AMERICA?

It is a common characteristic of both business and government today that a complex hierarchy of administrators is needed to translate policy decisions into executive action. It is, moreover, a common belief that the professionalization of administrators gives promise today and will eventually guarantee that the persons concerned with translating decisions into action will do so in a spirit of impartial service, whatever the nature of the policy involved.[1] The preceding chapters have indicated that in the American setting such background factors as social origin, education, and previous career-lines fail to show a homogeneity of administrators as a group that might conceivably militate against such impartiality.

Such indirect evidence is obviously insufficient. It needs to be supplemented by an examination of the institutional setting which bears on all efforts at professionalizing the civil service and which puts the achievement of administrative neutrality to a test. Unfortunately, the literature dealing with this problem fails to give the guidance that is needed. In view of the anti-bureaucratic, or perhaps anti-governmental, tradition of America, a good deal of the popular and of the scientific writing in this field has been devoted to an exposition of the bureaucratic evil and of possible remedies for it. The simple exposure of administrative shortcomings alternates with discussions of managerial correctives and a defense of the administrative process against judicial encroachment.[2] But the question remains: What factors have a bearing on the relation of bureaucracy in its invidious sense to the exercise of power?

Is it possible for the administrator to exercise his authority by delaying undesired decisions while speeding up the others through subtle discriminations in the treatment of his "clientele," by transforming the spirit of his enabling statute while following its letter, and by many other means? The answer is clearly that it is possible. But is it necessary? Is this the consequence of the large size of the executive agencies? Or is the discretionary exercise of authority desired by the administrators for the realization of their own ends? The social characteristics of higher Federal administrators are not uniform and the single-minded abuse of

---

[1] It should be added that this view has been modified in some instances in the light of recent historical experience. Professor Leonard D. White has qualified a strict construction of the idea of administrative neutrality by stating "that a career lawyer or a career administrator when faced with policies that the career man believes will yield social chaos or the destruction of constitutionalism, has no alternative. He must insist upon advice which will avoid these evils and if he is overruled he has no alternative but resignation." (Quoted from private correspondence with permission of the author.)

[2] These types are illustrated respectively by John H. Crider, *The Bureaucrat* (Philadelphia: J. B. Lippincot, Co., 1944); J. M. Juran, *Bureaucracy: A Challenge to Better Management* (New York: Harper and Brothers, 1944); and James M. Landis, *The Administrative Process* (New Haven: Yale University Press, 1938).

authority through bureaucratic machinations is not in that respect a plausible inference. On the other hand Federal administrators have many problems and interests in common and many of them desire to have their status as professionals recognized. The question remains whether the work-experience and professional aspiration of Federal administrators create among them the social cohesion and common outlook which has characterized, for example, the higher civil service in England or in pre-Hitler Germany.

An analysis of the "working climate" of the higher Federal service encounters obvious difficulties. It has to characterize the administrator at the center of a network of relationships with sufficient attention to the general features to convey an over-all view and with sufficient detail to show that typical situations are a living reality. Generalizations about the working relationships of several thousand people are hazardous and the instances cited in their support are selected by one observer. The attempt is made here, nevertheless, because the mass of available material makes even a first step worth while.

The intergovernmental relationships to which the administrator is subject, which he helps to form and to perpetuate, are very complex. Only three of these relationships are here selected for consideration. The higher administrator is concerned

  (a) with running his organization in such a way that it will readily respond to his directives;
  (b) with seeing to it that the agency will respond readily enough (but not too readily) to the demands made upon it by its "public";
  (c) with holding the activities of his agency within the limits defined for it by statute and maintaining effective relations with the Congress.[3]

T heserelationships constitute in part the frame of reference for the everyday operations of the administrator. It will be useful to discuss each of them in turn.

INTRA-AGENCY RELATIONSHIPS

Students of public administration are generally agreed that the administrator should possess, to quote one respondent, "an inherent ability to select, train, and lead his own organization to work with the subject and the people affected." Formal accounts of the problem of personnel selection in the Federal service tend to describe the rules and procedures of the Civil Service Commission and to set these in contrast to the spoils system. Useful though they are, they do not touch upon problems of major importance in actual government operations. For example,

---

[3] Left out are contacts with state and local governments, the problem of foreign relations, the whole problem of the relation between Washington and the "field," and so on. Moreover, many aspects of the problems cited in the text will be ignored, either because the writer is not sufficiently acquainted with them or because only rumors, but no reliable information, are available. It is hoped that the discussion may be useful as the over-all view of an outside observer, even if its coverage is only partial.

personnel officers may work to the detriment of efficient government administration when they substitute their judgment for that of the official under whom future appointees will work.[4] But this reference to a certain professional narrowness of some personnel officers hides a major problem. If personnel officers regard their methods of testing as superior, operating officials tend to regard personnel officers as an unfortunate nuisance. Says one of them: "I cannot understand what these personnel people are good for. If I need a particular man for a job, I send his papers up to the personnel officer, and he O.K.'s them, I suppose. I never have any trouble." Similarly, Dimock has given an account of how the personnel selection for the War Shipping Administration was regarded as unorthodox by the Civil Service Commission and was cleared only after prolonged negotiations. Such experiences can be multiplied, primarily with reference to the higher Federal service. They support the view that the Civil Service Commission is in effect concerned with seeing to it that the merit system is not violated. Its role in the selection of executive personnel is, therefore, predominantly passive.

I am not concerned here with an appraisal of the Commission. It is of interest, however, to observe the actual, if informal, working relationships which fill the interstices of the Commission's regulatory framework. Personnel selection in the higher Federal service for instance, is a matter of personal contact, professional association, and group interest. Some respondents emphasize the importance of "being around the right place at the right time to get the call on assignments." Setting up a new agency or bureau depends a good deal on staffing it with the right personnel. Inevitably the success of the undertaking will depend in large part on the comprehensive familiarity of the directing official with qualified persons in and out of the government service. Moreover, the prestige of an administrator is considerably enhanced if he can appoint his man (and even if he can appoint somebody else's candidate), quite apart from other considerations. Since an agency depends upon the teamwork of its personnel, there is obvious merit in the very informality of this recruiting procedure.[5]

But it entails problems as well. Some observers of the Washington scene have the impression, for instance, that certain employees in the higher brackets of the Federal civil service ("the bright young men") manage to utilize their contacts throughout the government in order to transfer every year or two to another agency, improving their grade or salary in the process. Our data on interagency transfers in the higher service suggest that this is an exaggeration. Yet the fact

[4] Dimock, *The Executive in Action*, p. 31.

[5] *Ibid.*, p. 35: "If a key-assistant's abilities are already known, the executive may proceed with greater assurance. This is so important that it goes a long way to offset the civil service insistence that everybody on an eligible list be considered before selection takes place. The most important requirement of civil service is appointment on the basis of merit. But a pre-existing relationship which assures teamwork and smooth operation is an element which cannot and should not be overlooked." (Reprinted here by permission of the publisher, Harper and Brothers.)

that such an impression exists is symptomatic. It points to the role of contacts in the day-to-day treatment of personnel problems in the federal service.

In the lower brackets of the Junior Professional appointees these contacts may in part account for the specific "university concentrations" which Lewis B. Sims has noted for the different professions among them.[6] That they play a role among the higher professional employees is indicated by the observation of one of them

TABLE XXX

Number and per cent of degrees received by respondents at different universities

University attended	Number of degrees received	Per cent
Harvard	36	11.2
Georgetown	22	6.9
Columbia	16	5.0
George Washington	14	4.3
University of Michigan	13	4.0
University of Wisconsin	9	2.8
National	9	2.8
Cornell	7	2.2
University of Washington	7	2.2
Washington College of Law	6	1.9
University of Chicago	6	1.9
University of Missouri	6	1.9
Johns Hopkins	6	1.9
Princeton	6	1.9
Iowa State	6	1.9
University of Virginia	5	1.4
University of Texas	5	1.4
University of Illinois	5	1.4
University of California	5	1.4
Stanford	5	1.4
Columbus	5	1.4
All others*	117	36.3

* The degrees comprised in this item have been acquired at eighty-one different universities (with from one to four degrees granted by each of these institutions).

that "most of the important officials of this agency have attended the University of Wisconsin and have been connected with the same WPA project." In this connection it may be of interest to tabulate the "university concentrations" of our sample of higher Federal administrators.

[6] Information on this point is contained in the study by L. B. Sims, *The Scholarship of Junior Professional Appointees in the Government Service* (President's Committee on Civil Service Improvement; Washington: Government Printing Office, 1940). See also Sims' summary of his study in his article, "Professional Personnel in the Federal Government," *Public Administration Review*, I (Spring, 1941), especially p. 274.

It is worth noting in this connection that the order of frequency in attendance is not substantially affected, if only the higher degrees (rather than all degrees) are taken into account.   Roughly the same universities were most frequently attended by such a group as the Foreign Service, which is in many respects widely different from the administrators sampled in this study.[7]   On the other hand, a considerably different attendance record is found among the employees of the relatively professional bureau to which reference was made earlier.   Although Harvard is still among the most frequently attended universities, such other institutions as Chicago, Syracuse, Wisconsin, and Minnesota rank much higher in the list.

These similarities and discrepancies are not revealing.   What is needed is an agency-by-agency survey of the educational background and occupational experience of professional employees in Washington.   In this connection the question of university attendance among higher Federal administrators is important for the light it may throw on the biases of recruitment in different agencies and for the possible effect of such biases on the clustering of certain types of personnel in particular government agencies.[8]   If such clustering exists, it is probably facilitated and perhaps enhanced by the many personal contacts which professional associations afford.[9]

This consideration is of importance, if it is placed in the context of day-to-day agency operation.   Personnel selection through contact in professional circles (inside as well as outside the government) may tend to develop patronage of a different kind.   The comment of one respondent is illuminating in this connection:

We are faced with a bit of a problem at the moment, in the field of public administration.   Most of the early specialists in this field were associated with institutions and universities financed by conservatives.   Under the New Deal a lot of younger administration specialists were taken into the government.   Thus, certain agencies "pushed back" certain of their older employees of high personal integrity and introduced many younger, more progressive employees.

Such a comment reflects the problems which result from a rather sudden influx of younger specialists into the higher grades of the civil service.   It suggests, in

---

[7] The following figures have been made available to the writer through the courtesy of Mr. Frank Roudybush from his unpublished study of 820 Foreign Service Officers: Harvard, 111; Georgetown, 78; Yale, 66; Princeton, 62; George Washington, 58; Columbia, 45; University of California, 32; Stanford, 29; Tufts, 23; University of Virginia, 22; University of Michigan, 20; University of Chicago, 18; Cornell, 16; and so on.

[8] An insight into what is involved here, from the standpoint of the universities, is afforded by the Hearings before a Subcommittee of the Committee on Civil Service, U. S. Congress, Senate, concerning S. 3450, "To Prevent Discrimination in Legal Appointments and Promotions," 75th Congress, Third Sess., April 20, 1938, in which a number of Presidents of smaller law schools protested against the discrimination in government appointments, from which their graduates feel they suffer.

[9] This inference is supported by our data on membership in professional associations among higher federal administrators.   Our data are insufficient, however, to throw light on the question of "university concentration" by agency. The number of cases for any one agency is too small, if it is remembered that such concentrations, if they exist, could be expected only in a specific bureau, not in an entire agency.

addition, that differences in age and training may be the basis for the creation and perpetuation of cliques among higher Federal administrators.[10]

While little systematic evidence is available to assess the importance of this factor, comments on it are so frequent as to suggest its significance for intra-agency personnel problems. Constructive leadership of an administrative agency depends for its success on the *esprit de corps* of its personnel, particularly in the higher brackets. Such leadership is obviously impaired, if subordinates are tempted to circumvent lines of authority and have the possibility of doing so with impunity. This covers a whole range of problems from invidious small-talk to enlisting Congressional support for a subordinate's point of view. It involves the problem of maintaining intra-agency morale in the face of a wide variety of predispositions which a miscellaneously recruited personnel cannot be expected to lose upon entering the civil service.[11] Such predispositions are strengthened through the continued contact of higher Federal administrators with their former professional and business colleagues. In most cases there will be no question concerning the loyalty of the administrator to his agency. But such contacts in themselves pose, nevertheless, a formidable problem for intra-agency teamwork. A good deal of weight should be attached, therefore, to the observation, frequently made by Washington officials, that a proposed policy may have great merit but that they doubt whether the administrator will be able to "sell" it to his agency.[12]

The problem of teamwork, which is aggravated by the absence of an administrative career service,[13] is not synonymous with the inevitable intra-mural conflicts of ideas and personalities which exist in any agency. The specific problem of teamwork in the Federal service is rather that intra-mural conflict which results from the effect of outside influences on the selection of an agency's personnel and on the work-relationships within. The problem is aggravated by the low prestige of the civil service (in so far as it still exists), which puts teamwork to many severe tests. There is, nevertheless, a premium on intra-agency solidarity against other agencies,

[10] It may be added that the respondent concluded the section of his statement quoted above by saying that "today there is need for emphasis upon character and integrity in the public administrator as well as for continued emphasis on professional training." The respondent entered government service in 1935.

[11] The problems for policy-implementation which these contacts create will be discussed subsequently. Although instances substantiating informal lines of communication between subordinates and private groups as well as the Congress have been mentioned in conversation with Washington officials, this is not the place to relate them in detail. In the nature of the case this is inside information and consequently difficult to check. Moreover, most instances which might be cited as illustrating subversion of authority may also be mentioned as illustrating an administrator's legitimate responsiveness to public demands.

[12] Actual control of superiors over their subordinates should be viewed in the light of two considerations: (a) good personnel management and the possibility that a Civil Service Commission might authorize a transfer of a dismissed employee (although the decision of the supervising official is final) set a certain premium on getting along; (b) there is evidence to substantiate the frequent comment that the bulk of the dismissals consists of transfers to other agencies. Littlejohn's study of P-1 appointees bears this out indirectly; the role of the Commission in this respect is not known to the writer. Easy opportunities of transfer do not set a premium on cooperation as far as the subordinate is concerned and would make the control of the administrator over his organization more tenuous.

[13] This phrase refers to the informal methods of personnel selection and the continued contacts of subordinates outside the government service mentioned above.

the Congress, and in a sense the "Great Public" (as distinguished from specific interest groups).   This solidarity is defensive because the body politic sanctions the actual participation of various interest groups in the administrative and the legislative process.[14]   Both a yielding and unyielding attitude towards "the public" is, therefore, part of the American bureaucratic culture-pattern.

THE ADMINISTRATOR AND HIS PUBLIC

If it is characteristic of the "Great Public" (as against specific groups) in America that it is remote and prefers to be aloof from the administrative process, it is just as true that Americans as individuals and in groups participate to an unusual extent in its operation.   In one instance the Weather Bureau found itself hamstrung in the promotion of the weather forecaster in a middle-sized town in Pennsylvania, which would have involved his transfer to another post.   The local protest against his removal was so strong that his promotion could not be made effective.   In another case similar protests from the people affected prevented the retirement of an employee.

Such stories would be of little interest by themselves, were it not for the fact that they illustrate the peculiar proprietary attitude of the American public towards its officials.   There is a sense in which government employees are regarded as the hired hands of the public.[15]   Thus the doctrine of the separation of powers is incorporated in the written constitution, but not, to use Professor Charles E. Merriam's happy phrase, in the unwritten attitude of the people.   It is a standing complaint of Congressmen that they are far too much burdened with administrative chores to fulfill their legislative responsibilities.   Yet politicians and political scientists are quick to emphasize the idea that such is the inevitable feature of a genuinely democratic government.   They share with many the conviction that the public should not only be concerned with, but should participate in, the administrative process as well as in the deliberations of the legislature.

For these reasons administrators frequently regard it as unwise to select persons for strategic administrative positions who are not acceptable to the particular groups with which the agency is concerned.   Moreover, it is unlikely that appoint-

[14] It should be clear from the context that there is nothing invidious in these contacts, but rather that this is a typical situation which the administrator confronts.   Of course, the problems arising for the internal organization of an agency depend a great deal on the character of the personnel involved as well as of the groups inside and outside the government with which contacts are maintained.   In many instances these contacts are no doubt salutary; in others they are without effect on the administrative process.   Moreover, the contacts range in character from continued business relations of an administrator to membership in professional associations.   And here in turn some professional associations are purely technical or scientific, others are academic with emphasis on research, and still others combine professional and trade association characteristics (*e.g.*, the bar associations).

[15] And on occasion civil servants endorse that attitude, although this particular view of public service was perhaps more frequent before the depression.   See, for example, the autobiographical account of Matthew F. Halloran, *The Romance of the Merit System* (Washington: Judda Detweiler, 1929).   The same attitude is reflected in the comment of one long-time observer, who regards the younger generation of civil servants as "power-hungry," in the sense that they place the merits of the policy which they help to administer on a level with the idea of service.

ments to the higher Federal service will go unscrutinized. In terms of service to the public the consideration has merit that the person administering a given program must be acceptable to the groups concerned. But by the same token it becomes questionable whether this form of public participation in the administrative process will allow an agency to pursue a consistent policy with regard to the public as a whole (as distinguished from interest groups).

One respondent writes:

> To be a successful administrator a man must have a thorough knowledge of the thinking habits and problems of the public affected by his administration, a sympathetic, deep knowledge of people and their reactions.[16]

Yet where should the administrator draw the line between a thorough understanding of his "public" and a yielding attitude towards various requests emanating from individuals and interested groups? The latter attitude is well illustrated in the testimony of Commissioner Foley before the U. S. Senate Banking and Currency Committee. Although nominally the subordinate of the Housing Administrator (John Blandford) and as such pledged to support the government policy on consolidating the various housing agencies, Foley testified in effect that the private housing groups served by the Federal Public Housing Authority were opposed to this amalgamation. Thus, in arguing the "case for his clientele" the Commissioner was in effect attempting to preserve his agency as a separate organization. In an instance of this sort it is difficult to distinguish the government administrator from the representative of a trade association within the government service.[17]

It should be emphasized, however, that the acceptance of public participation in the administrative process makes such actions legitimate. It gives, moreover, point to the observation that the important distinction does not lie between private and public employment but that the government service falls into a number of functional divisions. This view implies that the various government agencies stand midway between the government and interested groups in the sense that there is close contact and collaboration between the "housing people," or the "welfare people" or the "railroad people" regardless of their status as private or public employees.[18] This relation may take the form of mobility of personnel be-

---

[16] The other two traits of a successful administrator listed by this respondent are (a) a thorough technical knowledge of his subject and (b) the inherent ability to organize and lead his agency. This second point of his statement was quoted earlier.

[17] Cf. U. S. 79th Congress, 2nd sess., *Senate Document No. 1592*. Wagner-Ellender-Taft Bill. Part I of Hearings, November–December, 1945. Testimony of Commissioner Foley, especially pp. 158 ff., 166–167.

[18] Exceptions to this rule are the lawyers and administrative experts whose qualifications can be effectively used in divergent lines of private as well as public business. But such mobility of personnel across functional lines is narrowly circumscribed because the emphasis of all government agencies is heavily on specialized training. This is indicated by the importance which the Civil Service Commission gives to its tests of special competence. It is even reflected in the experience of administrative technicians, whose mobility across functional lines in the government service is the result of a new type of specialization, such as personnel work. Cf. Rowena Bellows Rommel, "The Making of Administrators," *Public Administration Review*, II (1942), 113–115.

tween private and public employment within these special fields; but this is not the factor of central importance.   Rather, government agencies and their respective private organizations constitute a forum for the discussion of national policy-issues. Such relations between an agency and its "special public" are significant because of their recognized bearing on policy formation.

It should be noted that the group-participation in the administrative process is not confined to the regulatory commissions or the so-called interest-departments (Commerce, Labor, and Agriculture) but pervades the activities of the executive branch as a whole, with the exception of only a few, highly technical services.   In this connection it has been stated

... that when the legislature finds it inadvisable to define specifically for future situations the content of the "public interest," the political problem of achieving consent to the application of such standards is passed on to the administrative agency.[19]

During the last fifteen years, at least, the legislature has found it increasingly difficult to do anything more than indicate the general purpose of its enactments.   As a result it has been left to the executive officials to take such steps in organizing an agency and facilitating the cooperation of its "clientele" as they deemed necessary. The political problem of achieving consent has, therefore, become the problem of the administrative process as a whole, rather than only the problem of the regulatory commissions.   As a result of this shift in the separation of functions it has now become incumbent both on the legislature and on the executive to obtain what consent they can.   It would be surprising indeed if such a development had not led to acute feelings of uncertainty concerning their respective functions in both branches of the government.

This uncertainty leaves the higher Federal administrator in a peculiar predicament.   It has always been his role to satisfy the demands made upon his agency by its "public."   But it is one thing to satisfy such demands and quite another to reconcile conflicting demands.   The latter function requires that the agency cultivate its public relations, use various forms of publicity to make its rules and actions known, and actually develop its contacts with various interested groups in the attempt to effect a minimum agreement on proposed actions.   It is not surprising that such activities have led to a twilight zone of the administrative process, in which the vaunted neutrality of the public service verges upon the struggle for power.

How is the administrator to combine these various roles?   In answering this question for himself, he must reconcile the following lines of action:

(a) He should execute the will of Congress as defined by statute.

19 Avery Leiserson, "Interest Representation in Administrative Regulation," *The Annals* (May, 1942), 80.   (Reprinted here by permission of the Editor.)   Cf. in this connection Leiserson's *Administrative Regulation* cited earlier and E. Pendleton Herring, *Public Administration and the Public Interest* (New York: McGraw-Hill Book Co., 1936), pp. 17–43.

(b) In the absence of specific instructions he should issue such rules as will effectively implement the legislative purpose.

(c) For this purpose he must cooperate actively with interested groups.

(d) Yet the work of his agency affects many such groups, who are as a rule at
cross-purposes one with the other.

(e) He therefore faces the additional task of developing such agreement among
them as the circumstances will allow.

(f) To this end he must engage in activities which will develop within the affected
groups an active interest in the operations of the agency.

(g) It would be surprising if the administrator would not point to the necessity
of his agency's continued operation, supported as this contention is by the
testimony which the interested groups render.

(h) In view of his new role as conciliator, the administrator will in all likelihood
be convinced that without his aid less agreement anong interest groups
would exist.   Effective policy implementation is conceived as the result of
agency operation, which creates agreement, which in turn supports agency
operation.

The political function of creating consent becomes fused in the mind of the
administrator with the desire (on his part and on that of the interested groups) to
perpetuate the agency as long as it succeeds in effecting agreement.   This is a
schematic picture in which the reciprocal relationship between agency and interest-
group is attributed to the partial transfer of the "politics of consent" from Congress
to the administrator.   But this new function of the administrator is not only
incumbent upon him when Congress is technically not in a position to specify its
intent or when the legislative inability to procure agreement transfers the problem
of achieving it to the executive.   It is well known that the initiative in matters of
policy formulation has been shifted in many instances to the President.   This
shift has created for the higher Federal administrator still another problem in his
relations to his "public."

As a member of the executive branch he is clearly committed to follow Presiden-
tial leadership in questions of policy.   On the basis of executive orders and other
more or less formal policy directives it becomes his task to enlist what public support he can obtain for a given policy.   It will be observed that the emphasis here
has shifted away from the function of obtaining agreement of various groups with
the broad intent of Congress and the specific rules which serve to implement it.   As
long as the administrator is the mediator between groups, his role is still passive.
But when he becomes the agent who initiates a new policy, he changes from the
executor into the advocate of a policy.   And in this role he is bound to reflect the
tensions which exist between the President and the Congress.   It is in this context
that the remark is pertinent that the administrator tends to regard the execution of

a policy as synonymous with service to the public. A number of officials comment to the effect that they are interested in doing their job as they conceive of it but that they would leave immediately if they were kept from doing it. Others express their dissatisfaction with the increased size of the Federal service because it makes a specialized function out of the task of fitting individual projects into a larger policy framework. That deprives the public service of one of its peculiar satisfactions.

But more important than the problems of individual motivation is the fact that the administrator as mediator and as advocate must become concerned with the problem of power. For example, the Congressional liaison man of an agency indicated that his major concern was not with explaining the work of the organization to the members of Congress. Rather he attempted to help various private groups in organizing themselves adequately and in defining clearly their own group aims regarding the functions of his agency for the purpose of bringing effective pressure on the Congress. Indeed, although the groups he worked with had hardly anything in common, he had been successful in having them agree on the program of the agency. The form of creating agreement between interested groups may not be the same in many cases, but many federal executive agencies are in various ways driven to similar activities.[19a]

Interest groups are not the only "public" with which the administrator has to deal. Other agencies in the executive branch are a "public" in the sense that the administrator must cultivate his relations with them, over and above what is required by the law. Hence, one of the outstanding features of public administration is the practice of "clearance." Accordingly, a former Washington official stated that the art of the administrator does not consist so much in making the right decisions as in the ability to make other people do a given job. This is an overstatement, but it points to the importance of coordinating the activities of the executive agencies. The same point is brought out in the whimsical comment of another Washington official, who said to the writer:

Secretaries are distinguished from administrators by their ability to obtain pertinent information from their files without delay. Administrators find it to be more time-saving if they obtain their information over the phone from other administrators.

Conversely, administrators find that it is more expedient to observe the lines of authority between different agencies than to cut corners by contacting their superiors.

[19a] In another instance the agency in question was actively engaged in public-opinion research as well as in programs of community education. That is to say, it was concerned with showing that public opinion was favorable towards its activities and with creating favorable public opinion. Indeed, once the policy was decided on, both activities were not only legitimate but necessary to its success. Yet it cannot be denied that both activities involved the agency in the struggle for the distribution of power.

But these everyday experiences do not touch the heart of the matter. Executive agencies which function in part as mediators and conciliators of conflicting group-interests cannot coordinate their activities without attention to their "publics." In fact, the instance of the housing agencies cited earlier would indicate that their effective coordination depends in part on the public support which this administrative measure receives. Coordination of Federal agencies may falter, however, when the conflict between different interest groups remains unresolved, each pressing its agency into action. This difficulty is aggravated if the conflict of interests has been incorporated by the Congress in its statutory enactments, whereby the problem of achieving consent is formally shifted from the legislative to the executive branch.

CONGRESS AND THE ADMINISTRATOR

The preceding discussion has been concerned with the relation of the higher Federal administrator to his agency and to his "public." Yet in almost every instance it touched upon his relation to the Congress. That is in accordance with the traditional conception according to which the Congress is the fountainhead of executive authority. But this traditional conception is not in line with the relative influence of the executive as against the legislature on policy formulation. Much attention has been given to the declining power of Congress, as compared with that of the Executive. Various institutional devices have been suggested in order to restore the power of the legislature. This is not the place to examine any of the excellent proposals for streamlining the Congress so as to make it into an effective instrument for supervising the administrative exercise of authority. Better staffing of committees, reorganizing the committee system, informal consultation between legislators and administrators—these and many other suggestions have been advanced before a Joint Committee on the Organization of Congress.[20] Most of these suggestions are useful. But none of them are sufficient to effect the reorganization of the legislature; none of them touch such fundamental problems as those posed by the seniority rule or by the position of the Rules Committee.

The legislature cannot in addition to the law-making process supervise the manner in which its enactments are administered.[21] However, it seems to be the practice of the legislature to see to it that the execution of its mandate will not result in a diminution of its power. But that involves Congressional supervision of administrative agencies. This supervision is an integral part of the struggle for power between the legislature and the executive. Such a statement does not imply

[20] The volume of Hearings before this Committee will be referred to subsequently as "Hearings on Reorganization."

[21] This is in accordance with classical liberal doctrine. John Stuart Mill writes that "the only task to which a representative assembly can possibly be competent is not that of doing the work, but of causing it to be done," and "the proper office of a representative assembly is to watch and control the government." In the same context Mill speaks of the assembly as "the nation's Committee of Grievances and its Congress of Opinions." See his "Representative Government," in *Utilitarianism, Liberty and Representative Government*, pp. 237–239.

an indictment of American politicians. It indicates only that it would be against their interests as politicians to relinquish this detailed supervision of administrative agencies. The politician is as subject as any other professional in the modern world to the peculiar mixture of blindness and vision which Veblen called "trained incapacity." His very expertness in the political struggle entails incapacities which administrators can disregard only at their peril. It will be useful to give a brief review of the Congressional setting.[22]

For each of the six Congresses from 74th to 79th an average of just under 80 per cent of the members were past their first term. During the same period the average tenure of all the members of the House was three terms, or six years. These data are supplemented by the tenure record of the members of various important Congressional Committees. During the 79th Congress members of the House Rules Committee averaged 4.6 terms; of the Ways and Means Committee, 4.4 terms; of the Appropriations Committee, 3.9 terms; and so on. If it is remembered that the failure to be re-elected for only one term puts a Representative again at the bottom of the seniority list, irrespective of his length of service prior to the interruption, it becomes obvious that the major job of the Representative is to obtain re-election.

It is not an exaggeration to say that this situation preys on their minds. Said Representative Coffee in his testimony before the Joint Committee:

Most of us are not prepared to go out to see our home folks often enough. It often happens that after several years up here some friends come to us and call us by our names and talk about old times, and we cannot recall their names. That is embarrassing to us, and it is a psychological hazard, because the Member is constantly impressed with the fact that he is losing touch with his home constituents, whereas his prospective opponent is able to spend days and nights going around to huskings in his own behalf. The Member is constantly upset with that worry....

One might say that is purely selfish—the political success, the tenure in office—yet it is a career. The average Member is here on the basis of a career. Most of the men with whom I am familiar are not here with the idea of any glory or glamor which may accrue to them, and they certainly are not here because of the compensation which they receive. Most of them could receive as much or more certainly in their private fields of endeavor. Most of them are motivated by an honest desire to lighten the burdens of the people at home and to render effective public service, and to the extent that their minds are clouded with worries about these attacks and lack of contact with the people at home, just to that extent is their undivided attention to public interest weakened and eviscerated.[23]

Congressmen are confronted with the necessity of giving their major attention to re-election. Only if they succeed in this can they hope to make politics a career. Only then can they acquire seniority and thereby the right to sit on important committees. If they cannot acquire status in the House, they will not become

---

[22] I am greatly indebted to John Eberhardt, fellow of the Social Science Research Council, for allowing me to read his unpublished manuscript dealing with an analysis of the Congress. Such specific data as are contained in the following paragraph are taken from his MS with his permission.

[23] *Hearings on Reorganization*, pp. 322–323.

known; if they remain anonymous, they will not be able to acquire status in the House. It is not surprising, therefore, that the majority of the members remain aloof from the law-making process, although the work-load is sufficient to keep all of the members busy all of the time. In fact, it is one of the paradoxes of the seniority system that the members are primarily concerned with obtaining re-election and seniority until they have acquired the latter. From that point on they will be so busy with legislative activity that they are continuously worried about whether they will be re-elected, since they do not have enough time to mend their political fences.[24]

Consequently, a great deal of the testimony before the Joint Committee was concerned with reducing the work-load of the Congressmen, especially their services to constituents. It may suffice to refer here to the comments of Representative Ramspeck:

> I endorse the suggestion that we need more competent assistants in our offices, but I venture the suggestion, Mr. Chairman, that all of that will not solve our problem, because you cannot get away from the desire of the constituents to see his Senator and his Congressman personally, and therefore you will not be able to share with an assistant a great deal of the burden that now exists because of the expansion of the Federal Government. . . .
>
> Therefore, in thinking what could solve the problem, I am going to make a suggestion which I say to you is quite drastic. Some of my friends have already told me it is politically a mistake to do it because they said people would get the idea that you do not want to do the job that you are elected to do. It is not that. All of us like to do things for our constitutents. We like to be able to go to the Post Office Department and get a rural route extended, or the city delivery route extended a block. We like to go to the Federal Works Agency and get a project for our district or for our State. . . . But we cannot do those things and do an intelligent job of legislating under present conditions. . . .
>
> There are just not enough hours in the day to do this job and to do both of them right—*the job of legislating and the job of representing the people before the executive branch of the Government.* Since you cannot divide yourself, the only other answer I see is to divide the job, to take away from the legislative Representatives any right to participate in things before the executive branch, and then give that job to another person elected for that purpose.[25]

Representative Ramspeck gave the issue a neat formulation; but his friends were perhaps more realistic. It is hardly possible to separate this form of representation from the legislative function so long as the public itself regards them as of equal significance. And it is important to note that the Senators and Representatives are on the whole in agreement with that point of view. At the same time they are thoroughly harassed by the unconscionable amount of time which is spent in

---

[24] Dr. Eberhardt's study contains a detailed analysis of the legislative activities of the members in the House. Among other matters, it brings out in detail the relation between seniority and legislative activity, and the importance of solid election districts (The South and the Northern Cities.)

[25] *Hearings on Reorganization*, pp. 296–297. (Italics mine.)

"Representation before Executive Agencies." It is of interest to note the comment of Senator White on this problem:

> ... one of the difficulties under which we are laboring ... is a confusion in the public mind between legislative responsibilities and administrative obligations. To illustrate, you have spoken of O.P.A. ... The difficulty is they (the people) may approve the law we have passed even though it is in general terms (*sic!*), but then they expect us to deal with every particular decision that O.P.A. has made. ...
>
> We lay down the general provisions of law, ... we indicate our purposes, and then it becomes an administrative task to carry those out. But I venture that there is not a day of our lives that we do not have ten or a dozen requests to do something about some administrative act which we recognize clearly is not a congressional act, is not a legislative responsibility. I do not know how to avoid the impact of that situation.[26]

But the members of the Congress do not only struggle with a staggering workload in their attempt to be both legislators and representatives in this sense. They also come into an equivocal relation to the administrator. As legislators they lay down the law; as "representatives" they seek in some way to alter its application from what it would be without their intercession.[27] The people do not recognize that Congressmen represent them through their legislative activity. And the Congressmen find it difficult to retain their legislative perspective while they are engaged in a quasi-administrative and quasi-lobbying activity. Congressmen realize that they may at times become favorably disposed toward an agency which served them well and on occasion adopt its point of view.[28] And many of them have little chance to acquire a perspective of national problems because their endeavors to serve the people back home and to get re-elected force them to neglect their legislative responsibilities.[29]

Re-election is the source of their power. To acquire that power Congressmen feel that they must represent their people before the executive branch. But to exercise that power the same Congressmen must enact the laws and supervise their execution. In the law-making process they again represent the people whose de-

---

[26] *Ibid.*, pp. 505–506. See also the comment of Representative Monroney: " ... we are in fact legislators; we make the laws; we don't administer them, and yet, when a break-down in administration occurs, the people naturally look to their legislators for relief or the correction of an intolerable condition. This throws us across a line which we shouldn't be thrown across, mixing into executive operations, but we are forced to, whenever the administrative functions seem to a reasonable constituent to break down and demand action by an extracurricular method." *Ibid.*, p. 621.

[27] It is not suggested that Congressional interference with the administrative process involves illegal acts in any sense. But the member's expectation of administrative service to him and the administrator's anticipation of Congressional censure are bound to result in liberal allowances being made in the application of administrative rules.

[28] *Hearings on Reorganization*, p. 297 (Rep. Ramspeck), and p. 157 (Rep. Priest).

[29] In this connection Rep. Ramspeck commented on his experience as Democratic whip of the House. He found that "very few" of the members even read the bills and that it was difficult for him to pursuade them to take on legislative responsibilities. As is well known, the people back home do not pay much attention to the law-making process.

mands they seek to incorporate in the enactment.   As Senator White pointed out, the people may agree with the general law, but not with its specific application. Congressional supervision of the administrative process is likely to be as haphazard as are the demands which the Congressman represents in his legislative and lobbying activities.   While Assistant Secretary of State, Dean Acheson stated this case before the Joint Committee:

> In order to deal with these problems (of the modern world) Congress has necessarily had to enact broad statutes which grant very considerable powers with a great deal of discretion to give rule-making authority and adjudicatory authority to administrative agencies, and those agencies then have had to hammer out their policies within that framework of Congress.
>
> Now, when Congress has done this, most of the subjects have been controversial, so that Congress has only half, or a little more than half, believed in what it was doing.   It knew it had to do it, but it knew it did not like to do it, and having done it, it wanted to draw back what it had done.
>
> . . . Having given broad authorities to administrative agencies, then they say these are tyrannical, these are very bad.   So a Committee investigates them.   Congress having realized at the outset that the agencies must have broad powers, immediately tries to withdraw the broad powers by reviewing through the committee the most minute decisions, taking up sometimes individual cases that had been decided, going over all rules that are made.   As the heat of battle grows on that front, it is transferred to the Appropriations Committee, and, instead of financing the organization which it has created for better or for worse, it begins restricting it by minute provisions in the Appropriations Act.[30]

It may be added that Congress not only withdraws its own grant of power soon after it has been made but also makes inconsistent or contradictory grants of power since neither the processes of re-election nor the functions of legislation and representation set a premium on consistency.[31]

Re-election and representation do set a premium, however, on the benefits which the people secure from their Congressmen, since these benefits constitute the indirect source of their power.   The battle between Congress and the administrator, of which Mr. Acheson speaks, turns, therefore, on the question whether the direct contact of the politician with his "public" and his direct services to it are being undermined by the administrative process.   That question was in the mind of one respondent, who emphasized the view that

> . . . the quality of administration depends on the type of men who have entered the public service. This is the key to the future, but I hope you don't overlook this factor as applied to politics, since that in turn tremendously affects the quality of administrations.

[30] *Hearings on Reorganization*, p. 499.

[31] The view that the politician has the role of effecting compromises does not give sufficient attention to the possibility that (a) Congress can pass on the unresolved conflict through contradictory enactments to the executive branch, and (b) Congress can undo its own compromise, which was incorporated in the law, by interfering piecemeal with its administrative application.   "Politics as Compromise" is discussed in Leonard D. White and T. V. Smith, *Politics and Public Service* (New York: Harper and Brothers, 1939), pp. 237–247.

However, in his contact with the Congress the administrator does not simply deal with individual members and their idiosyncrasies and political preferences. He is, rather, confronted with the "occupational psychosis" of politics as a career.[32]

The testimony before the Joint Committee contains a striking number of assertions, both from Congressmen and from administrators, that it is the job of Congress to legislate and to supervise the administrative process. It may be inferred that the repetition of such an obvious truism indicates a feeling of uncertainty on the part of the members.[33] This feeling is based on two facts. First, few members of the House have detailed knowledge of the laws on which they vote. Second, the supervision of administrative operations must be conducted by Congressmen whose knowledge of the subject is that of the layman.[34] The feelings of uncertainty which result can lead to petty questioning and criticism, to ill-concealed aggressiveness, and to many statements *vis-à-vis* the administrator which are helpful in bolstering Congressional self-confidence and prestige.[35] Moreover, widespread neglect of legislative in favor of "representative" tasks as well as the feeling that Congress is powerful in name but not in fact aggravates the doubts of many Congressmen about their own role. But all of these phenomena of "occupational psychosis" are the symptoms of a struggle for power, which find their counterpart on the administrative side.[36]

Administrators emphasize their feeling that much of the difficulty arises from lack of time, which makes it next to impossible for them to serve the Congressmen well. In many instances it is necessary to examine all the evidence bearing on a

[32] This concept of John Dewey is discussed in Kenneth Burke, *Permanence and Change* (New York: New Republic, 1936), pp. 54–70. Note particularly the following passage (reprinted here by permission of the publisher): "Any performance is discussible either from the standpoint of what it *attains* or what it *misses*. Comprehensiveness can be discussed as superficiality, intensiveness as stricture, tolerance as uncertainty—and the poor *pedestrian* abilities of a fish are clearly explainable in terms of his excellence as a *swimmer*." Thus, politician and administrator will be fully alive to their own attainments, but they will develop a peculiar blindness or "trained incapacity" in their appreciation of each other's attainments. They will be acutely aware, on the other hand, of each other's shortcomings.

[33] In fact, one Representative told this writer that in his judgment the bad relations between administrators and Congressmen were to be attributed to feelings of inferiority on the part of the latter. Although he did not specify the reasons for such feelings, he did state that they frequently led to unconsidered actions and an ill-advised slashing of funds of specific agencies.

[34] *Hearings on Reorganization*, pp. 707–708; 155–156.

[35] The Hearings before the Joint Committee brought out repeated assertions that administrators are really men of good will, indicating that this point must frequently have been in question. The testimony contains also a great many statements asserting that Congressmen really mean to fulfill all their obligations conscientiously, that they work hard, and that their various acknowledged shortcomings are no fault of theirs.

[36] I am passing over the many comments and suggestions of Congressmen and administrators which regard the difficulties of their relation from the point of view of better public relations. An official emphasized to the writer the idea that there is need for more cocktail parties which would give both parties a chance to meet informally. Many outstanding Federal officials (like John Blandford, Chester Bowles, William A. Jump, and others) emphasize the view that there should be frequent informal consultation between executive officials and the respective supervising Committee. Still others remark that the basic difficulty lies in the lack of mutual confidence and respect between the politician and the administrator and that much of this problem is solved whenever the administrator happens to have had political experience. (This point is reminiscent of the Congressional criticsm of administrators, who "never carried a precinct or met a payroll.") Most suggestions along these lines are helpful; few if any touch on the major problem.

case before arriving at a decision, since premature judgment may create untold complications later on.   But Congressmen frequently insist on having an immediate decision and complain about red tape and inefficiency.   To be sure, it is possible to refuse Congressional requests if care is taken that the reasons for such refusal are pointed out.   But on the whole Congressmen show little understanding for the characteristic problems of the administrative process.   And although some requests can be refused, the misconceptions remain.[37]   It is not surprising, therefore, that administrators frequently anticipate more blindness in the Congressional approach to administrative problems than actually exists.

Moreover, administrators find themselves frustrated when confronted with a Congressional failure to effect a compromise.   This situation may take the form of authorization for two agencies to operate in the same field,[38] or it may become evident in the enactment of contradictory policies.   Large-scale integration of governmental agencies tends to increase such frustrations, because it frequently prevents the higher Federal administrators from presenting the case for their bureau to Congress.   The presentation of an entire departmental program may create the feeling that a better case could be made for a specific agency.   Such feelings are of importance among administrators who view their work in a professional light.[39]   Also many problems arise for administrators because Congressional and public criticism points to the shortcomings of their actions without adequate appreciation of the more serious drawbacks of alternative decisions.   For instance, congressional criticism forever points to "bureaucratic delays."   Yet, as one official pointed out, the "administrator must spend a third of his time in justifying

[37] In his testimony Chester Bowles criticized the fact that contact between agency heads and the Congress occurs only when critical issues are at stake.   He failed to mention the fact that only on such issues can Congress exercise its supervisory functions.   Otherwise Congress would have to duplicate in miniature all executive agencies.   Where Congress has attempted to exercise retrospective control in detail, such as through the General Accounting Office, it has resulted in continuous friction with the executive branch.   See *Hearings on Reorganization*, p. 729.   See also the comments of Dean Acheson, who points out that publicity is always given to controversy but not to smooth-working relationships between Congress and the Administration.   (*Ibid.*, pp. 501–502.)   But the problem may be that Congressmen and administrators react to each other just as the Press does, noting the critical issues and distrusting or neglecting the wide areas of successful cooperation.

[38] Such duplication has hitherto always been explained as "bureaucratic aggrandizement," when one agency—contrary to the intent of Congress—seeks to usurp the activities of another.   Although there are instances of this sort, insufficient attention has been given to the case mentioned in which Congress passes on an unresolved conflict to the administrative branch.   If authority is given to one agency only, the administrator is concerned with reconciling conflicting interest groups.   But if it is given to two agencies, the conflict between such groups is transformed into a conflict within the executive branch.   Although it is extremely difficult to assess the importance of such problems, it would be unwise to dismiss such considerations on the ground that the evidence in this area is elusive.

[39] In addition, the inexpertness of Congressional inquiry and supervision increases the temptation to evade curtailment of activities which are regarded as essential by intra-agency manipulation.   Instances have been cited to the writer in which agencies have asked for more money than they would need for the next year in anticipation of congressional cuts.   (Undoubtedly, the Budget Bureau has substantially reduced, if not eliminated, such practices.)   Cuts in appropriations for a specific activity have sometimes been evaded by transferring the number of people affected to a different division, where they continued their previous work.   Congressmen comment to the effect that some budgetary offices will abolish in their estimates such divisions as are sure to be put back into the appropriation by Congress, whereas they will retain the items which have come in for Congressional criticism.

what has been done and what is being planned for the future" for the sake of satisfying the Congress.[40]

The areas of conflict, in which these predispositions of Congressmen and of administrators become manifest, are many; clearly not all are of equal significance. It may suffice to call attention to the problem of government publicity. To the Congressman close contact with "the people back home" is the source of his power. To the administrator close contact with the special public of his agency is the basis of efficient operation. In a hearing before the House Appropriations Committee, J. C. Capt, Director of the Bureau of the Census, cited in his general statement concerning the estimate for 1947 several letters indicating public support of the Bureau's work. He was interrupted in his testimony at one point by Representative Gillespie. Part of their discussion follows:

Mr. Gillespie: Let me ask a question right there. How did you get those letters?

Mr. Capt: The Bureau and the Department sent out to business concerns, trade associations, chambers of commerce, and so forth, a program asking their advice, counsel, and recommendations as to the program and, in response to that invitation to criticize and make suggestions for improvement or realignment of our activities, we got back these replies.

Mr. Gillespie: I do not know how the rest of the Committee feel, but, as far as I am concerned, you do not need to read any more testimonials. We can figure those things out.

Mr. Capt: We can figure those things out, too; we did not get testimonials; we got advice. We sit in Washington and we cannot possibly get in touch with everybody on a program of this character and, after discussing the program with interested Governmental agencies and the Bureau of the Budget, and the people we can get to locally, we still wish to have, and seek out, the advice and counsel of people who cannot come to Washington. And the best way we can get at that is to send in writing what we propose to do, to as many individuals, firms, chambers of commerce, and trade associations we may know about.

Mr. Rabaut: Supply for the Committee, but not for the record, a copy of the letter you sent to those people.

Mr. Gillespie: Not only that, but these are no good to us unless you let us see all of the letters you received. If you let us see all of the letters you received, that is one thing, but just to let us see the ones you picked out does not mean anything to me.

Mr. Capt: They were selected at random and represent a fair cross-section. You probably think there were some that were adverse, but the number of adverse letters we got was insignificant. It was a small number, but I will gladly send them to you if I can find them.

Mr. Gillespie: But you do not have any of them in there?

[40] In such comments there is a noticeable impatience with the conditions of administrative work. If the major emphasis is on getting things done it is obviously frustrating to delay for the purpose of giving an account of what is being done. On the other hand, if the major emphasis is on the representation of interests and the control of authority by a representative body, the time devoted to making the action of the administrator accountable is spent wisely. Clearly the administrator has difficulty in appreciating the importance of supervision exercised over him, whereas the legislators find it difficult to remember that their supervision of the administrator partly causes the inefficiency which is the object of their criticism. Such are the "trained incapacities" which hamper legislators and administrators alike. Of considerable interest in this connection is a German Ph.D. dissertation by Kaethe Truhel, *Sozialbeamte* (Sagan: Benjamin Krause, 1934), in which the "occupational psychoses" of social case workers and welfare administrators in German municipalities are analyzed. Cf. also the article by Robert K. Merton, "The Role of the Intellectual in Public Bureaucracy," *Social Forces*, XXIII (May, 1945), 405–415.

Mr. Capt: No.

Mr. Rabaut: Here is the proposition: It is all well and good to be alert as to what you think should be done, but it ought to be up to the Congress to create the work for the Departments, and not have every corner of the universe writing in to the Departments and telling them what their functions are; what they ought to be doing; what they think about this; what they think about that, with a suggestion from the agency. Congress ought to run the country.

Mr. Hare: Where is Congress going to get its information?

Mr. Rabaut: Congress gets its information from the people and then calls the agencies and talks to the agencies about suggestions that have been made to them. There is nothing wrong in getting information, but there is hardly a place you can stop.[41]

There are surely other instances in which the dispute between Congressman and administrator is conducted more amiably. But this excerpt aptly illustrates the basic problem which government publicity involves.

Politicians are sensitive to the fact that administrative agencies have direct contact with the public. Congressmen denounce such contact as propaganda. At the same time they deny that administrators have any real knowledge of what the people want. (If administrators did have this knowledge they would thereby jeopardize the "representative" function of the politicians.) In this connection Congressmen have pointed out that the publicity of "Departmental Washington" is not the full story and that information emanating from government agencies is largely self-serving. Only Congress provides an opportunity for debate and the presentation of conflicting points of view.[42] Consequently, the publicity of administrative agencies appears to Congressmen as in effect (even if inadvertently) undermining the popular belief that the elected representatives provide services for the "people back home."

Many proposals have, consequently, been made with the purpose of bringing the story of Congress to the people, so that they will look up to and respect it as an institution. According to the view of Representative Coffee,

Congress has been badly represented to the people in the public press and on the public platform. . . . Every Federal department and bureau in Washington, with few exceptions, has a press-relations section. Their job is to represent that bureau or department favorably to the public and give their story out in the press and over the radio. But Congress has never seen fit to retain that public-relations division, and the only way we can be defended is when the Speaker of the House or the President of the Senate, or now the President pro tempore of the Senate, or majority or minority leaders see fit to give some statement in the general defense of Congress as an institution, and even they have their statements discounted, because the public knows they happen to be Members of the body and may speak with prejudice.[43]

[41] Hearings before the House Committee on Appropriations, Department of Commerce Appropriations Bill for 1947. U. S. House, 79th Congress, 2nd Session, January 30, 1946. Testimony of J. C. Capt, Director, Bureau of the Census, pp. 247–248.

[42] Cf. the testimony of Senator White in *Hearings on Reorganization*, p. 736

[43] *Ibid.*, pp. 320–321 (testimony of Representative Coffee).

Statements such as this are evidence of a struggle for power, which cannot but affect the administrative process. They pose for the higher administrator the problem of operating effectively in a climate of suspicion. They manifest the anxiety of some Congressmen that administrators and the people at large hold them in contempt.

The remaining discussion will deal with the bearing of this climate on the conduct of administrators and with some of their attempts at gaining recognition as a professional group.

CHAPTER IX

CONDITIONS OF ADMINISTRATIVE CONDUCT

The findings of the preceding discussion may be summarized as follows:

(a) There is no evidence to indicate that higher Federal administrators in the United States are homogeneous either in social origin or in educational experience.

(b) Evidence does indicate that since 1933 the persons entering the government service have been recruited increasingly from professional groups or from among persons with graduate training.

(c) The incentives which prompted them to choose government employment have been mixed. The circumstance that government salaries compared favorably with professional salaries (if not with those of business executives) undoubtedly played a role. But part of their reason for entering and much of the reason for staying in the government service was a desire for participation in large-scale programs for the general welfare and, perhaps, subsequently, a desire for personal identification with the public service.

(d) There are important, if diminishing, differences between business and governmental administration. Controls over business decisions are very indirect (for example, consumer's choices). Government administration is, on the other hand, continuously subjected to various forms of supervision.

(e) The "working climate" of Federal administrators is noticeable for the complexity of checks emanating from intra- and inter-agency relations, from the "publics," and from Congress, to which their activity is subject. An outstanding characteristic of this climate is the difficulty of pursuing a consistent course of administrative action in view of the necessity of anticipating demands for special considerations as well as the continuous scrutiny of administrative acts.

What does it mean to say, under these circumstances, that the administrator seeks to be neutral? One anser to this question is negative and legalistic. The administrator does nothing which contravenes the intent of the Congress as incorporated in statute. Neutrality in this literal sense is not, however, neutrality in fact, since Congressional enactments are for the most part so broad as to make an administrative interpretation of the Congressional purpose necessary for its realization.

Another answer is suggested by the attempt to distinguish between administration and policy formulation. The neutral administrator confines himself to a purely advisory function, stating his judgment when called upon to do so, but executing the policy decided upon however much it may be contrary to his own beliefs. This view of neutrality overlooks the fact that the distinction between administrative (or technical) advice and policy determination is a textbook truth. Questions of policy are involved whenever a subordinate defers to his superior for a decision.[1] Policy decisions are made throughout an administrative hierarchy; deferring to superiors becomes less and less feasible the higher the administrator is placed. Moreover, no administrator is ever exclusively concerned with the techniques of management, since managerial expertness is applicable to the execution of any policy decision. Administrative actions, however technical, cannot be divorced, therefore, from the political culture-pattern of which they are a part.[2] The administrator is not neutral merely because he is an expert; rather, his neutrality depends upon the development of a professional ethic.

A third conception of administrative neutrality is that the administrator should make himself the accurate sounding board of the "antagonism of influences" which emanates from his own organization, the "Great Public" as well as various interested groups, the Congress, and the President. This is the least meaningful conception of administrative neutrality.[3] By yielding to each group in turn the administrator would have no policy to follow. Yet compromises are achieved; administrators do strike a balance between conflicting influences and adhere to lines of policy, however blurred these may be at times.

These three definitions of neutrality in the public service are frequently combined in the literature, so as to suggest that adherence to statutory limitations, proper distinction between administration and policy formation, and adequate responsiveness to superior authority make up the meaning of neutrality. It may be suggested, however, that these three definitions are more the reflection of political philosophies and historical trends than the formulation of a code of administrative conduct. The idea of an administrator who is a strict constructionist of his enabling statute conforms to the adage that democratic government is a "government by laws and not by men."[4] The administrator, on the other hand, whose advice is sought and who is technically proficient, whereas his judgments on policy issues, if he has any, are confined to his private thoughts, is the ideal of the expert. His claim to be recognized as an expert rests on this strict construction of his professional ethics. Finally, the administrator whose official actions reflect the va-

[1] Statement made to the writer by Mr. Herbert Emmerich, Director of the Public Administration Clearing House Chicago.

[2] Cf. in this connection Harold D. Smith, *The Management of Your Government* (New York: McGraw-Hill Book Co., 1945), pp. 28–29 and David M. Levitan, "The Neutrality of the Public Service," *Public Administration Review*, II (1942), 317–323, and "Political Ends and Administrative Means," *Public Administration Review*, III (1943), 353–359.

[3] This view is easily ridiculed in the sense that the conception of neutrality which each group favors most would have the administrator be responsible to the group in question. But it is perhaps more accurate to say that in the commonly accepted view the influence of other groups or agents (like the President or Congress) is acknowledged, although it is true that each in turn would have the others play a minor role.

[4] For a discussion of the historical origin and the political uses of this slogan cf. Jerome Frank, *If Men Were Angels* (New York: Harper and Brothers, 1942), pp. 1–21, *et passim*.

riety of pressures to which he is subjected is the idol of those who identify democracy not with the freedom of each to speak his mind and advance his cause, but rather with the idea that each individual and group is entitled to have its demands fulfilled. Government in this view becomes the twentieth-century replica of Jacksonian Democracy, not in the sense that the majority but rather that everybody is entitled to a proportionate share of the spoils.

This historical involvement of the administrator suggests that the factors which have shaped his conduct may be analyzed (a) in the light of the profound suspicion of the Federal administrator which is an important legacy of American historical experience and (b) in relation to the attempt of administrators to become a professional group. That attempt may entail forms of conduct because of this prevailing suspicion which deviate from professional norms in order to achieve recognition for them.

CIVIL SERVANTS AS AN UNDERPRIVILEGED GROUP

Earlier studies have shown that people have little esteem for public employment or public employees.[5] Our previous discussion has suggested, however, that this attitude may have changed since the late 1920's. Government salaries compare favorably with salaries in private employment. The Federal government is a source of employment and of initiative in large-scale projects. In this sense it has established confidence in its projects and by assuming an increasing variety of roles has engaged the people's imagination. But although the prestige of government may have increased, there is no evidence to indicate that the public attitude toward the Federal administrator has changed fundamentally. The increasing use of publicity by Federal agencies helps, of course, to diminish both the remoteness and the anonymity of the Federal official. Yet, even if there are a few heroes among our administrators, most of them are still the hired hands of the public.

Federal administrators receive less recognition than employees who are otherwise comparable in terms of training and specialization, because they are not accepted as professionals and because their legal status marks them out as an underprivileged group. This legal inferiority seems predicated on the assumption that civil servants are under special obligations to the government as their employer without compensating safeguards or privileges. This position of the civil servant is closely related to a conception of democratic government which expects the administrator to render faithful service to all the groups interested in his field of activities. As long as each group thinks itself entitled to a proportionate share of government activities in its behalf, it will expect the agent of the the public (the administrator) to give unstinting service without thought of his own interests. This view of administrative service is not a formulated doctrine which guides public conduct.

---

[5] See the studies on the prestige of public employment by Leonard D. White cited above, p. 11, n. 26.

It is rather the ideological and legal precipitate of a multiplicity of public actions toward government.   As we have seen, the ambivalence of the relations between administrator and public is a constant source of irritation for the relation between legislature and administration.   This ambivalence of the status of the civil servant is intensified whenever the public and the legislature charge him with new responsibilities.   Every new grant of authority increases both his prestige and his power and at the same time intensifies the suspicion that he will abuse them.

Restriction of the civil servant is not, of course, a specifically American phenomenon.   All the democracies of Western civilization have enacted laws regulating the activities of the civil servant in and out of office, particularly with regard to political affairs.[6]   But whereas other governments have relied upon general rules reinforced by a tradition of impartiality, as in Great Britain or in Republican Germany, the emphasis in the United States has been placed on a specific enumeration of the activities in which a public official may not engage.[7]   Moreover, the Hatch law provides that a Federal employee may express his opinion "on all political subjects and candidates," but shall not take any active part in political campaigns.   The law does not specify what expressions of opinion do not constitute such active participation.   But it is difficult to conceive how prominent Federal officials will be able to express their opinions without violating the law.   However, legal provisions and public agitation against the political activity of civil servants are but a nineteenth-century remedy for a twentieth-century problem.[8]

This criticism is not an argument that such provisions are superfluous.   But if Federal administrators wanted to abuse their power they could do so far more effectively through means which would be found unimpeachable under the Hatch law.   Here again it is not only the institutional arrangement but the cultural and the psychological impact of his "second-class citizenship" which is likely to influence the conduct of the civil servant.

It is significant in this respect that the whole effort of civil-service reform has been directed toward establishing the merit principle in the recruitment of public

---

[6] Cf. the article by Otto Kirchheimer already cited (above, p. 8, n. 12) and Fritz Morstein-Marx, "Comparative Administrative Law; Political Activity of Civil Servants," *Virginia Law Review*, XXIX (August, 1942), 52–91; and Herman Finer, *The Theory and Practice of Modern Government* (London: Methuen and Co., 1932), II, pp. 1374–1422 and chap. xxxiv.   See also L. V. Howard, "Federal Restrictions upon the Political Activity of Government Employees," *American Political Science Review*, XXV (June, 1941), 470–489.

[7] Morstein-Marx, *op. cit.*, 84–91.   It should be added, however, that the tradition of civil service impartiality in Great Britain and in Germany was predicated upon the implicit recognition by all officials of a political *sine qua non* which exists perhaps as much among American administrators, although continued public suspicion of the contrary may well undermine it.   For a description of a successful maintenance of such a tradition despite the increase in government functions, cf. H. E. Dale, *The Higher Civil Service of Great Britain* (New York: Oxford University Press, 1942), pp. 136–139, *et passim*.

[8] An analysis of American wartime experience in this respect is contained in the article by Robert E. Cushman, "The Purge of Federal Employees Accused of Disloyalty," *Public Administration Review*, III (1943), 297–316.   The whole problem of the political neutrality of the civil servant is treated from the civil-liberty point of view by Wallace Sayre, "Political Neutrality," in F. Morstein-Marx, ed., *Public Management in the New Democracy* (New York: Harper and Brothers, 1940), pp. 202–217.

employees. That emphasis is clearly a reflection of the spoils tradition. But if much attention has been given to the elimination of partisanship from government appointments, considerably less attention has been paid to the elimination of abuses from the policies governing public employment. A survey of overtime records by the Civil Service Commission for the period from July 1 to December 31, 1936, indicated that 76,448 employees had worked overtime for 10,613,698 hours, or an average of 1,768,949 hours per month.[9]

Compensation for overtime work has been provided for in the meantime, at least for the lower brackets of the Federal service. Postal employees and workers in the trades and occupations were entitled to receive pay for overtime work in 1941. It was still true, however, that the superiors of employees in the departmental service "may, by special order, stating the reason, further extend the hours of any clerk or employee in their departments, respectively; but in case of extension it shall be without additional compensation."[10]

Although the policies governing the hours of work are in process of reformulation, the rules concerning the dismissal of employees are not; and, as they stand at present, they almost seem to invite abuse. As of 1941 the employee whose removal is under consideration is allowed to answer in writing the charges made against him. The removing superior has final authority except that he is required to give reasons and allow the employee sufficient time to answer them. The rules contain explicit provisions against procedural safeguards unless the removing official himself adopts them. This condition is, if anything, aggravated by explicit provisions against review of the decision of the removing officer by the Civil Service Commission. The Commission is, on the other hand, entitled to authorize on appeal the transfer of the dismissed employee.[11]

To one judging this aspect of government personnel policies only in terms of these formal provisions, it would appear that the authority of supervisory officials is limited by the possibility of transforming a dismissal into a transfer. There are advantages in charging superiors with the evaluation of the working performance of employees. But these advantages are lost if the Civil Service Commission is only able to transfer an employee, but unable to review his dismissal. A premium is put on appealing dismissals to the Commission once they occur. A premium is also placed on avoiding the dismissal of employees in the first place. The supervisory official will not want to acquire the reputation of unjustly dismissing employees; and a few transfers of employees whom he dismissed will earn

---

[9] This represents uncompensated overtime, and 50 per cent of it was on the part of employees receiving less than $2,000 a year. While the evidence is now partly out of date and some provisions for overtime pay have been incorporated in the Civil Service Rules, it is nonetheless symptomatic. The data are quoted from an unpublished report by the Commission in Carol Agger, "The Government and Its Employees," *Yale Law Journal*, XLVII (1938), 1124.

[10] U. S. Civil Service Commission, *Civil Service Act and Rules*, (Washington: Government Printing Office, 1941). pp. 239–240.

[11] *Ibid.*, pp. 104–105.

him this reputation. Moreover, he will feel reluctant to dismiss employees if he has any reason to expect that they will subsequently be transferred; in that case he might as well arrange for their transfer himself. The rules themselves seem to encourage both the legal inferiority of Federal employees and the inefficiency of the service. Both are aggravated by the difficulties of dismissing and the ease of transferring employees, which limit the effectiveness of personnel supervision.

Although their powers are curtailed in this way, supervisory officials must seek to enhance their own position and the good of the service by perfecting the working performance of their organization. One writer has commented on the situation as follows:

> Strongly actuated by a desire for advancement or for the added personal prestige which results from outstanding division records, supervising government officials behave in much the same fashion as many less enlightened private employers. The history of the Post Office Department, greatest of government industries, is replete with illustrations. Nor are others hard to unearth. The flimsy charge of inefficiency has shielded not a few dismissals of government employees because of union activity. Similarly, that perennial source of complaint for some industrial workers, the speed-up, has often plagued government employees, especially in such large semi-mechanical units as the Bureau of Internal Revenue, the Treasury and the Social Security Board. Dissatisfaction and unrest among employees were particularly rife in the latter department, where new supervisors were striving to enhance their own reputation by exacting the maximum work from their units. All too often the ambitious official, challenged by employees to readjust unfortunate conditions, takes refuge in the concept of "executive responsibility" and its supposed corollary that his authority brooks no interference. His reaction is not unlike that of the business man who "will not be told by any damned union how to run his business" and proceeds from the same unconscious emotional bias. Indeed, the government official is more fortunate in that "executive responsibility" sounds so much more important and mysterious.[12]

This description should be somewhat discounted since the author of the passage is a strong advocate of trade unions among government employees. It is true, on the other hand, that as of 1939 only three departments and three independent establishments of the Federal government had instituted formalized grievance procedures, and of all Federal executive employees (outside the Post Office) only 19 per cent were trade-union members.[13] Moreover, the rules governing dismissals suggest the presence of ambivalent incentives, which alternately encourage and frustrate effective personnel supervision. As a result it seems reasonable to infer that the conditions of public employment combine the legal inferiority of public employees with an uncertainty of supervision, which inadvertently has the effect of vacillating between indulgence and exploitation.

---

[12] Carol Agger, *op. cit.*, p. 1110. (Reprinted here by permission of the publisher.)

[13] For further details and a comprehensive discussion of the whole problem see Gordon R. Clapp and others, *Employee Relations in the Public Service* (Chicago: Civil Service Assembly, 1942), pp. 16–17, 122–123, *et passim.* Cf. also Fritz Morstein-Marx, "Comparative Administrative Law: Public Employer-Employee Relationships," *University of Detroit Law Journal*, IV (January, 1941), esp. 61–68, 86–90.

DILEMMAS OF ADMINISTRATIVE CONDUCT

Such evidence indicates that the American Federal administrator is at a disadvantage in his legal status and personal freedom as compared with persons in similar positions in private employment. These disadvantages are coupled with an atmosphere of suspicion and frequent defamation, which cannot make this "second-class status" any easier to bear.[14] Yet, and here we return to the crucial problem, it is these men whom the people and their representatives have entrusted, however reluctantly, with a great deal of discretionary authority. In the last resort only the administrator can decide how this authority may be exercised in a reasonable manner. How have our "second-class citizens" responded to this first-class challenge? Case studies of government agencies could provide specific answers to this question; but they could not overcome the defects of the microscopic approach. On the other hand, an over-all evaluation of the setting of public administration does provide an answer. That answer, too, is defective in many respects, but it has the virtue of indicating typical variants of the administrator's approach to the exercise of his power. The three notions of administrative neutrality, which were mentioned earlier, may serve as a useful guide.

"Under a perpetual glare of Congressional criticism" and faced with public suspicion and denunciation, administrators have in many instances adopted a narrow construction of their functions. Their major concern has been with questions of legality and with the examining of each administrative task in the light of the limits which the enabling statute prescribes. Such execution of legislative policies is the administrative equivalent of public suspicion of all authority, which Gunnar Myrdal regards as a characteristic American attitude towards government. Even though it is paradoxical, administrators themselves have often adopted this popular attitude, which combines veneration of the law with suspicion of its application. Some believe, moreover, that special consideration should be given to the circumstances of the individual case, since the acts of administration do not partake of the sanctity of the law. As Senator White has observed, people will agree with a general law but oppose its administration in specific cases.[15]

The legalistic administrator is akin in action, if not in spirit, to his more adaptable counterpart, who believes that an administrator should be of service to the people, should be guided by the President, and should follow Congressional direction. Both approaches to the problem of administrative discretion are under-

[14] In fact, many administrators express considerable irritation at the offhand manner in which their venality is taken for granted by the public.

[15] Cf. the observation of James Bryce that the main features of American government can all be deduced from two principles: the sovereignty of the people and their distrust of government and its officials. The demand for special consideration of individual cases follows from the first principle, and the strict supervision through various checks as well as the frequent suspicion and denunciation of officials indicates the validity of the second. See James Bryce, *The American Commonwealth*, (New York: The Macmillan Co., 1910), I, ch. xxvi, esp. pp. 305-311.

standable forms of administrative defense.   Both are designed to protect the administrator from the public criticism which he knows to be inevitable.   In both cases he can point to the legal rule or to the superior command which prompted his action.   Both types of administrative behavior indicate a desire for security which the conditions of public employment in America are likely to intensify.

In view of the conflicting directives emanating from the public, the Congress, and the President, administrators seek the stability which is inherent in a departmental policy.   In this way they may be able to safeguard a conscientious adherence to the enabling statute or to preserve the procedural efficiency of the agency. Any of the so-called bureaucratic devices may be serviceable to that end.   Red tape, for instance, may be used to make sure, and doubly sure, that the proper legal safeguards are observed.   This strict adherence to enabling legislation can be put into effect in such a manner that policy-determining officials are unable to modify it.[16]   Administrators, on the other hand, who are persuaded that they should respond to various conflicting demands still have to get their work done. To that end they must protect the regularity of their procedures and the consistency of their official conduct.   Futher, bureaucratic manipulation may help them to counteract the disrupting influence of conflicting pressures and to avert or at any rate to mitigate the insecurities which result from it.   Red tape, for example, as well as the inevitable delays of administrative procedure may be used to prevent an insistent pressure group from achieving its particular ends.   Bureaucracy in its invidious sense may, therefore, be interpreted as an administrative defense about which such notions as neutrality or bureaucratic usurpation of power are beside the point.[17]

Administrative legalism and the administrative equivalent of "spoils-democracy" are not the only bases of bureaucratic manipulation.   The attempts to professionalize the civil service are equally on the defensive, although they aim at improving the inferior status of civil servants and at gaining recognition for a code of professional conduct.   The efforts to organize the manual and clerical personnel in Federal employment take the form of unionization.   Professionalization of civil servants, on the other hand, is concerned with technical and professional employees.   Both types of organization are well characterized by the formulation

[16] For a description of this kind of bureaucratic manipulation cf. Dimock, *The Executive in Action*, pp. 235–240; also Arnold Brecht, "Bureaucratic Sabotage," *The Annals*, CLXXXIX (January, 1937), 48–51.

[17] Levitan has made a strong case for a distinction between administrative neutrality toward political parties as against neutrality toward the agency's program.   That administrators even in the lower brackets cannot be neutral in the second sense is indicated by the following example: "The policy incorporated in the act or the policy of any board may be very liberal, yet a group of procedure writers may include so many rigid conditions for filing claims, hiding behind the fiction that it is the business of the persons concerned to know all the requirements, that a great number of individuals may be deprived of payments although the act and the board intended that they should be compensated.   We are not speaking of conscious violations of the sipirt of the act, but rather of unconscious deviations on details of administration."   See his "The Neutrality of the Public Service," *Public Administration Review*, III (1943), 322.   (Quotation reprinted here by permission of the Managing Editor.)

of objectives contained in the original constitution of the National Federation of Federal Employees—namely, "To advance the social and economic welfare and education of the employees of the United States and to aid in the perfection of systems that will make for greater efficiency in the various services of the United States."[18]

To combat the inferior economic position and the ill repute of the administrator, it was necessary to associate his welfare with the ideas of economy and efficiency in the government service. Suspicion of administrators at times gave rise to the belief that any organized effort on their behalf was *prima facie* subversive. Consequently, Federal-employee unions as well as professional organizations of civil servants have repeatedly protested their loyalty. They have emphasized that they are primarily concerned with the reform of governmental administration, not with their own welfare. These organizations have, therefore, been an important part of the movement for civil-service reform on all levels of government.[19]

Professionalization of administration and concern with better government go hand in hand. So far, however, little emphasis has been placed on the problem which this partnership entails for the acceptance of a code of professional ethics among higher Federal administrators. The administrator who, as a professional expert, desires to implement given policy decisions cannot live up to his conception of his role so long as it is not accepted by the public at large. His efforts at attaining impartiality are in themselves politically controversial and his every attempt at professionalizing the civil service will necessitate his partisanship in behalf of impartiality.[20]

Futhermore, as long as his professional status is as yet not accepted, the administrator may be forced to use the devices of bureaucratic manipulation for the sake of practicing his professional ethics or of gaining recognition for it. For example, red tape may be used to make doubly sure of administrative impartiality—a defense which would be less necessary if confidence in this impartiality were widespread. This lack of confidence has other important consequences. It promotes the desire of administrators to have their claim to professional status reinforced through membership in professional associations. Contact with professional col-

---

[18] Quoted in Luther C. Steward, "Civil Service Unionism: a case in point," in F. Morstein-Marx, ed., *Public Management in the New Democracy*, p. 190. (Reprinted here by permission of the publisher, Harper and Brothers.)

[19] Cf. the commemorating issue of the *National Municipal Review* of November, 1944. I am also indebted to C. Herman Pritchett, of the University of Chicago, for permission to read his unpublished MS *1313: An Experiment in Propinquity*, in which the history of some professional civil service organizations is traced.

[20] Cf. for example, the recent hearings concerning the Bureau of Agricultural Economics, in which Dr. Tolley was severely criticized for having presented to the Secretary of Agriculture alternative policies on cotton prices. This fact was regarded as indicative that Dr. Tolley did not have the interests of the farmer at heart, which of course were identical with the policy advocated by the interrogating Congressman. See Hearings before the House Committee on Appropriations, Department of Agriculture Appropriation, Bill for 1947. U. S. House, 79th Congress, 2nd Session pp. 182–194, 202–205, 226–231. See also the detailed evaluation of these hearings by Charles N. Hardin, "The Bureau of Agricultural Economics Under Fire: A Study in Valuation Conflicts," *Journal of Farm Economics*, XXXVIII (August, 1946), 635–668.

leagues inside and outside the government will, among other things, fortify the self-confidence of administrators as professionals. It facilitates, moreover, the development of an independent judgment, which the prevailing suspicion of the administrator makes at the same time important for his professional work, difficult to attain, and questionable in the eyes of his critics.

These professional contacts, involving both personal ties and the possibility of exchanging ideas beyond the pale of unfriendly scrutiny, serve a double purpose. They promote government reform and aid the administrator in his attempt to acquire technical competence and to see it recognized as such. Civil-service reform and the professionalization of administrators are compatible. But as long as civil-service reform is attempted without recognition of administrators as professionals, they are likely to regard their professional ties as part of their administrative defense. It is interesting that the professional organizations of civil servants have adopted elaborate ethical codes but have failed to make membership contingent upon some test of professional competence. This fact stands in odd contrast to their insistence on the importance of scientific principles in public administration.[21]

Although there are serious doubts whether the existence of scientific principles is a guarantee of administrative neutrality, there is little doubt that this inference is convincing to the public at large. Moreover, administrators seek to counteract the presumption that they will abuse their authority by insisting that their work is based on scientific principles. The emphasis on science and on the importance of codes as well as the failure to test the professional competence of members may be the sign of the youth of the profession. But it is also a sign that this professionalization is an instrument in the struggle for recognition on the part of administrators. As such it prompts administrators to violate their professed code of impartiality. Administrators are reformers precisely to the degree that their impartiality is attacked and recognition of their professional standing withheld. It follows that they are not likely to be neutral as long as they are suspected of partiality; and their actions will not mitigate the suspicion. It may be asked whether full recognition of the professional competence of administrators and acceptance of their code of impartiality will turn them into conservatives.

The mainspring of administrative conduct in the Federal service is the necessity of reconciling the popular distrust of authority with the necessities of efficient administration. This distrust may be the cause of bureaucracy in its invidious sense and may distort the efforts of administrators to establish an impartial, professionally-competent civil service. Bureaucratic evasions are also a response to the continous questioning of policies whose implementation has been sanctioned

---

[21] Cf. John M. Gaus's comments on the observation that faculties teach at times more than they know concerning the principles of administration. See his *Research in Public Administration* (Chicago: Public Administration Service, 1945), pp. 153–161, 166–175.

through legal enactment.   The feeling of insecurity which results, plus the constant anticipation of checks on their activity, is likely to intensify the timidity of some, whereas it may prompt others to pursue within the broad limits of the law a policy of their own.   This whole gamut of degrees of administrative independence (ranging from timidity to a well-meant abuse of power) seems to develop equally from the desire to serve the public.

But the public speaks in many conflicting voices.   In order to serve this master the administrator must face the necessity of making government possible in the manner he thinks best, even through bureaucratic maneuvering amid the antagonism of influences, if nothing else avails.   If he is thereby prompted to exercise his authority in a more discretionary manner than would otherwise be the case, he is likely to say that this method is not of his own choosing.   If he violates the spirit of administrative neutrality, he does so with the idea of service to the public. The ideal of impartiality in public administration will be approximated in the United States only in proportion to a growing public recognition of its importance in the face of the forever-shifting struggle for power.   Failure or success in the development of a professional civil service is, therefore, contingent upon the developments of public understanding.

CHAPTER X

CONCLUSION

The preceding study of the public servant in American democracy has been concerned with three related topics: (1) the social homogeneity or heterogeneity of higher Federal administrators; (2) the elucidation of the American bureaucratic culture-pattern; (3) the problem of professionalization of the American civil service. The analysis of these topics may be conveniently summarized in the following propositions.

(a) American administrators come predominantly from rural areas and small to medium-sized towns.

(b) They come predominantly from lower middle-class and middle-class families.

(c) During the last generation a gradual shift has taken place, such that administrators come in decreasing numbers from farmer's families and in increasing numbers from professional families. The proportion of administrators coming from "business families" has remained relatively stable.

(d) A majority of the higher Federal administrators have acquired their college and graduate education through their own efforts.

(e) Although administrators have had diverse occupational experiences prior to their government service, some preponderance of businessmen, lawyers, college teachers, and journalists is noticeable.

(f) The common belief that the incentives of public employment compare unfavorably with those of private employment is unfounded except for top executive positions.

(g) The social origin, educational background, and occupational experience of administrators show considerable diversity. (This diversity stands in contrast with that of other professional groups, which may be as diverse in social origin but show much greater similarity in educational and occupational background.) Such uniformities as appear can be accounted for by reference to over-all developments—namely, the decline in the proportion of farmers, the increasing spread of high-school and college education, the growing skill requirements in the government service, and the specific demand for persons with legal training, experience in writing, and in organizational work.

(h) The bureaucratic culture-pattern in America consists in the unusually wide discrepancy between respect for law in the abstract, the demand for consistent government administration, and the profound suspicion of many administrative acts. This condition of the administrative process creates

121

specific occupational disabilities in the relation between the administrator, the public, and the Congress.

(i) Whatever the regard for government itself, its administrators suffer from a distinct lack of social prestige and, more tangibly, from a deprivation of specific rights and securities which private employees of comparable standing have attained.

(j) In their efforts to improve both the operation of government and their own position, administrators are attempting to organize as a professional group. This attempt has to reckon with the popular suspicion of the government official. As long as this is the case, administrators will have to grapple with the peculiar problem of adhering to the norms of professional conduct at a time when their claim to professional status is still disputed.

Administrators in America do not constitute a homogeneous social group. Although a majority of the higher civil servants have had professional training in a variety of fields and aspire to establish themselves as professional administrators, the evidence of this study does not indicate that they have as yet developed a common outlook. The diversity of educational and occupational background militates against it, as well as the circumstance that the popular suspicion of government administration calls forth a variety of defensive responses in the absence of firmly-established professional ethics. It is true that the similarity of problems facing administrators has promoted professionalization as part of the struggle for improving the material and social status of the civil servant. The full development of social cohesion among administrators as a professional group is, however, contingent on changes in the attitudes and actions of the public towards government authority.

APPENDIX

In the following pages are reproduced the letters and questionnaires used for obtaining data on the group of administrative officers sampled for the foregoing study.

THE UNIVERSITY OF CHICAGO

SOCIAL SCIENCE RESEARCH COMMITTEE

OFFICE OF THE CHAIRMAN

Dear Mr.

In cooperation with Professor Leonard D. White and Professor Louis Wirth of the University of Chicago I am making a study of the educational and occupational background of high officials in the U. S. government as of 1939/40. This study is supported in part by the Social Science Research Committee of the University of Chicago.

Studies of government in different countries have shown that the quality of administration depends on the type of men who have entered the public service. We hope to enhance our understanding of American government by acquiring, with your help, a more intimate view of the men who have risen to positions of importance in the administrative branch of our government. We ask you to check and return the enclosed form, even if you are not now in government work.

We have intentionally made the questionnaire as brief as possible, in order not to burden you unduly. It would be appreciated, however, if you would use the last page to give us your opinion on any point covered in the questionnaire or any other aspect of your experience with problems of administrative personnel which you feel might be of value to this study.

The questionnaire will be handled anonymously,

Your help in this study will be greatly appreciated.

Sincerely yours,

Reinhard Bendix

THE UNIVERSITY OF CHICAGO

SOCIAL SCIENCE RESEARCH COMMITTEE

Dear Mr.

A few weeks ago we sent you a questionnaire in connection with a study of the educational and occupational background of higher federal administrators. The response so far has been unusually good in view of the obvious difficulty which most respondents must have had in finding the time necessary for it.

We would, therefore, especially appreciate it if you could return the questionnaire in the near future, since we expect to begin our tabulations soon. Perhaps I should add that these background data are intended as part of a larger study which will be based on interview material as well as historical research.

Please disregard this request if you have already returned the questionnaire.

Sincerely yours,

Reinhard Bendix

Questionnaire

1. Date of Birth.............................. Place of Birth...
   City   State

2. Education (Circle only highest Grade attained):
   a) Grammar and High school, or Preparatory school: Public School.... Private School..........
      Grades completed: 1 2 3 4 5 6 7 8 9 10 11 12   Year of Graduation............

   b) College or Technical Institute: 1 2 3 4 year completed

      Name of Institution(s):..

   c) Graduate Work (Number of years): 1 2 3 4 5 6; Institution:..

   d)

Degrees received	Year	Institution	Field of Specialization
....	....	....	....
....	....	....	....
....	....	....	....

3. Occupational History: indicate in the following table the principal positions of your occupational career (other than government service) by specifying opposite each relevant category a) the length of time for which you held that position; b) the type of business, in which you were employed.

	From	To	Type of Business
Laborer (unskilled or semiskilled)........	....	....	....
Skilled Laborer (or mechanic)..........	....	....	....
Clerk or Salesman...................	....	....	....
Farmer.....................Owner	....	....	....
......................Tenant	....	....	....
Small Business (Sales under $50,000)			
Supervisor	....	....	....
...................Executive	....	....	....
...................Owner	....	....	....
Large Business (Sales over $50,000)			
Supervisor	....	....	....
...................Executive	....	....	....
...................Owner	....	....	....
Other Profession (specify):			
....	....	....	....
....	....	....	....
....	....	....	....

4. Career within the Civil Service:

Department	Title	From	To	Classification (e.g. CAF 13)
....	....	....	....	....
....	....	....	....	....
....	....	....	....	....
....	....	....	....	....
....	....	....	....	....
....	....	....	....	....

5. Have you ever been offered a position in private employment, since you have joined the government service? Yes........ No........ Indicate the type of business from which such offer(s) has (have) come:...

6. Place the names of associations to which you belong opposite the following categories:

   a) Social and/or recreational Clubs:...

      ....

      ....

   b) Business Associations:...

      ....

      ....

   c) Professional Associations:...

      ....

      ....

7. Indicate the *one or two principal* occupation(s) of your Father, your Father-in-Law (if any), your Brothers (if any) and your sons (if you have any who are employed full time). Check the following list:

	Father	Father in-law	Brothers	Sons
Laborer (unskilled or semi-skilled)......................				
Skilled Laborer (or mechanic)..				
Clerk or Salesman...........				
Farmer..............Owner				
..............Tenant				
Small Business (Sales under $50,000)...........Supervisor				
...........Executive				
...........Owner				
Large Business (Sales over $50,000)...........Supervisor				
...........Executive				
...........Owner				

	Father	Father in-law	Brothers	Sons
Other Profession (specify):				

8. If you have sons who are going to College, indicate:

Institution	Field of Specialization (if any)
....	....
....	....
....	....
....	....
....	....

9. Additional Remarks:..

....

....

....

....

....

....

....

THE UNIVERSITY OF CHICAGO

SOCIAL SCIENCE RESEARCH COMMITTEE

Dear Mr.

A few weeks ago we sent you a questionnaire in connection with a study of higher federal administrators (as of 1940). Although we have had a surprisingly good return (over 50%) we recognize that many could not spare the time to accede to our request.

As a result we have searched the various biographical sources (e.g., Who's Who, Contemporary Biography, etc.) for the relevant data. These sources are adequate with regard to educational and occupational data, but they do not yield any information on family background, or on offers of employment from outside the government. We are including, therefore, a one-page questionnaire, which may be filled out in a few minutes, and ask you to please return it to us. This will supplement what information we have already obtained from the sources mentioned above.

Your help in completing these data will be greatly appreciated.

Sincerely yours,

Reinhard Bendix

Questionnaire

Indicate the *one or two principal* occupations (during their lifetime) of your Father, your Father-in-Law (if any), your Brothers (if any) and your sons (if you have any who are employed full time). Check the following list:

	Father	Father in-law	Brothers					Sons			
Laborer (unskilled or semiskilled).											
Skilled Laborer (or mechanic)....											
Clerk or Salesman...............											
Farmer................Owner											
.... Tenant											
Small Business (Sales under $50,000.............Supervisor											
.............Executive											
.............Owner											
Large Business (Sales over $50,000)............Supervisor											
.............Executive											
.............Owner											

Other Profession (specify):

....											
....											
....											
....											
....											

Have you ever been offered a position in private employment, since you have joined the government service? If so, indicate the type of business from which such offers have come....................